School Librarians and the Technology Department

School Librarians and the Technology Department

A Practical Guide to Successful Collaboration

Mary Ann Bell,
Holly Weimar, and
James Van Roekel

 LINWORTH

AN IMPRINT OF ABC-CLIO, LLC
Santa Barbara, California • Denver, Colorado • Oxford, England

Copyright 2013 by ABC-CLIO, LLC

Library of Congress Cataloging-in-Publication Data
Bell, Mary Ann, 1946–
    School librarians and the technology department : a practical guide to successful collaboration /
Mary Ann Bell, Holly Weimar, and James Van Roekel.
        pages cm
    Includes index.
    ISBN 978-1-58683-539-2 (hardcopy : alk. paper) — ISBN 978-1-58683-540-8 (ebook)   1. School
libraries—Administration.   2. Educational technology.   I. Weimar, Holly.   II. Van Roekel, James L.
III. Title.
    Z675.S3B4525   2013
    025.1'978—dc23   2013006985

ISBN: 978-1-58683-539-2
EISBN: 978-1-58683-540-8

17 16 15 14 13   1 2 3 4 5

This book is also available on the World Wide Web as an eBook.
Visit www.abc-clio.com for details.

Linworth
An Imprint of ABC-CLIO, LLC

ABC-CLIO, LLC
130 Cremona Drive, P.O. Box 1911
Santa Barbara, California 93116-1911

This book is printed on acid-free paper ∞

Manufactured in the United States of America

Contents

CHAPTER 1

Looking Back:
How Far Have
We Come?

Introduction

Educators do not need to be told that technology is a large part of their working lives. Those who have 20 or more years' experience can take a look back at a fast ride from the tentative beginnings of computers in schools back in the 1980s to today's immersion in every aspect of education. As technology has increased in importance, teachers and librarians have seen dramatic changes in their jobs. Back in the early 1980s, there were relatively few computer teachers or technology specialists. If a teacher or librarian was interested in computers and technology, he or she self-educated, often through trial and error. There was a time when a mildly adventurous person could pop the top on an Apple IIe, reach down inside, and add cards or wiggle things around to fix a problem. Since teachers using computers were something of a rarity, such tinkering was sometimes the only way to make repairs or increase a computer's capabilities. Today there are technology educators on school campuses as well as in district positions. Educators in both positions are often overworked, and increasingly so in today's hard times. In order for their jobs to achieve optimum effectiveness, technology personnel need to work with librarians. In turn, librarians need to have good working relationships with all technology staff. Collaboration between librarians and technologists is not a hazy goal; it is a concrete and immediate necessity. This is even more of a must-do in today's challenging school climate where positions and equipment are often cut, especially if they do not show their value very tangibly. The purpose of this book is to explore ways to nurture and enhance strong working relationships between school librarians and all technology staff members, both campus and district, within the larger context of the entire school community. The intent of this book is to offer best practices and philosophical backgrounds to assist both librarians and technologists in working together to best serve all patrons: students, teachers, administrators, and parents.

In the Beginning

For most schools and teachers, the advent of computers in schools began in the early 1980s. Early on, computers found their way into district and school offices first, used for data entry and other business applications. In forward-thinking libraries, they began to see use for circulation management. Wide use of computers in schools was kick-started by the development of the personal computer. The most popular early PC was the trusty Apple II. Soon after that, people fell in love with the Commodore 64 (Figure 1.1), most popular personal computer of all time. During this time, Apple computers had a very strong hold on school computers, especially those used by teachers and students. There was an attitude among many educators that PCs were good for business and Apples were good for education.

During the 1980s, computers in school classrooms and libraries started out with students learning very simple programming. LOGO, created by Seymour Papert, gained interest and popularity. Soon after this, simple programs for teaching and learning began to spring up. Some of those that were popular were the following:

- Odell Lake
- Math Blaster
- Where in the World is Carmen SanDiego?

Meanwhile, it became increasingly apparent that teachers and students needed instruction that taught users how to operate these new-fangled computers. School districts began incorporating computer classes into their curriculums. In most cases, computer use was taught in isolation, in labs under the direction of computer teachers. Out of

Figure 1.1: The Commodore 64 computer was a popular choice of home PC users.

these beginnings grew a propensity for "drill and kill" software where students interacted only by providing answers to scripted questions, usually multiple choice, true–false, and so on. Early creativity beyond that might be said to be possible through word processing where children could be creative in their writing, or with simple drawing applications such as Apple's Draw or Windows Paint.

Apple was trying to maintain leadership by branching out into programs that allowed more creativity. The leap from AppleWorks to more interactive use was largely made by a watershed application, Hyper-Card, to be followed a bit later by HyperStudio. Both these programs allowed students to create content. They became wildly popular among educators who used them both for their own lesson creations and also to challenge youngsters to create original products. During these days, Apple continued to dominate, with the new software a major factor.

In the late 1980s, PCs began their push to be more prevalent in the lucrative school market. IBM was an early player as were HP and Compaq. Software started to emerge to compete with the increasingly extensive offerings by Apple. People started to think students should use PCs in school because they would need to be comfortable users after graduation when they took their places in the business world. As the Apple IIs aged out, many were replaced with PCs. The cost gap was another reason to make the change. By the end of the 1980s, the Apple/PC ratio of computers present in school was about 50/50 (Molnar). At the same time, computer use had increased in complexity. There were more applications from which to choose and more things that teachers and students could do using computers, regardless of platform.

The growing demand for the presence and instructional use of school computers gave rise to a new field for teachers to pursue: computer science. More and more schools had at least one computer teacher and lab. Districts began hiring technology directors to oversee training of users and management of equipment and software. From early days, librarians were called upon to join with technology teachers to maximize technology use on many campuses. Forward-thinking librarians and library directors embraced computer technology with enthusiasm.

Storage

How to store and share information and software was the next challenge. First attempts at information storage were 5-1/2 inch floppy disks (Figure 1.2) that became ubiquitous for use with both computer platforms. These offered program software and also allowed users to save their own data and move it around from one computer to the next. As with previous developments, this led to more and more use in new and different ways in schools. Before long, the dependable but limited 5-1/4 inch floppies, which really were a little bit floppy, began to be replaced by the smaller and not at all floppy 3-1/4 inch disks. These ruled the storage world of information and software well into the early 1990s.

Compact Disks

As was the trend with earlier developments, the growing body of information and program demands soon outstripped the capability of both the large and small floppies. New computers appeared that touted an even better storage vehicle, the compact disk or CD. This was a game changer in many ways. It allowed for a great deal more information to be held in one object, including images, sound, and film clips. Soon rewritable CDs gave users portability to move information and applications from one computer to another. *And* there was competition. Another development was the laser disk. Sized about the same as a

Figure 1.2: Floppy disks were widely used for storing data in the 1980s.

78-rpm record, laser disks, developed by David Paul Gregg at Pioneer, boasted both storage capacity and high-quality resolution of pictures and sound. Probably the best known laser disk software, which hit schools in the early 1990s, was called Windows on Science. Sets of these disks allowed teachers to share lessons, illustrations, and activities with unlimited combinations. Those trained to use Windows on Science were told that a major advantage was that the data were not sequential. The user could move from one point in the presentations to another without having to scroll through irrelevant content. Windows on Science remained in school use through the late 1990s with high user satisfaction. Alas, the laser disk did not fulfill its early promise. Size was one reason. Lack of programs other than and beyond Windows on Science led to its short-lived popularity.

Infrastructure

Tentative steps were made in the early 1990s to connect computers one to another rather than having all free standing. The term "networking" was bandied about. A very early attempt was AppleShare, which would allow several computers to be joined, thus enabling software used on one to be used on up to four. This was useful in libraries where CDs that allowed such use could be accessed by several students at once.

The watershed event that became the driving force behind the push for infrastructure was, of course, the Internet. Al Gore may not have invented it, but he recognized early on that infrastructure was imperative

Figure 1.3: Coax cables were instrumental in early computer networking.

if schools were going to reap the benefits of what was available via the Internet. Early wiring was achieved using coax cables (Figure 1.3). These were relatively inexpensive and easy to use, but sadly lacking for distances beyond the confines of one building and less and less capable of carrying the amount of traffic needed.

The next big leap forward was fiber-optic cable. In the mid-1990s, forward-thinking districts bit the bullet and paid for fiber-optic infrastructure rather than opting out in favor of buying other things with technology funds, including more computers. Then came Net Day, with the accompanying run-up and aftermath. The most widely publicized event associated with the term "Net Day" was March 16, 2006, when a number of California schools were connected with the assistance of thousands of volunteers. "It was a high-visibility event—even America's president and vice president joined in: 'Donning electrician's gloves and hopping on a ladder, President Clinton joined the cyberspace revolution Saturday as he worked with Vice President Al Gore to install about 70 feet of pink, white and blue conduit at a Contra Costa County high school,' " wrote the *San Jose Mercury News* (1996).

Growing Importance of Internet

Net Day was not without detractors. There were those who scoffed at the idea that connectivity, networking, and Internet access would live up to the hype. In the mid-1990s, the net could be frustratingly slow, especially during hours of peak use. Users in the first three time zones could tell when California reached maximum logons around midday PST because their own speed would drop noticeably. But with the advent of the Internet, a revolution had begun that would not be stopped. More and more schools, businesses, and households began to rely on the Internet for information, applications, and communication.

- This surge encouraged the trending toward distance education. While distance learning formerly was the bailiwick of the U.S. Mail, online learning began to span great distances with greater ease than heretofore imagined.

- Communication since Internet's advent has changed irrevocably. According to Harper, the term "snail mail" was coined to dismissively describe sending messages the old way. The origin of this term is hazy, but by the mid-1990s, it had close to universal acceptance. Indeed as early as 2000, a survey reported that for most business correspondence, snail mail had been eclipsed by email.

- Online full text information for educators and students exploded with the Internet's advent.

Importance of Technology Specialists and Librarians

As computers in schools moved from interesting frills to vital necessities, the demand for educators to help manage the growing plethora of hardware, software, and information became a challenge at all levels from early childhood to higher education. Who would keep track of and keep running all these new computers and peripherals? Who would train users, both students and faculty? Who would bring a sense of order to the glut of information and help separate the wheat into the chaff? The average classroom teacher was overwhelmed with other duties, especially as the new trends toward high stakes testing evolved. Two groups of educators came to the front: technology specialists and librarians. It is worthwhile to look back at the development of educators in these two roles over the last 30 or so years.

Technology Specialists

Back in the 1960s and 1970s, campuses did not have technology teachers. Technology comprised the tried and true 16-mm projectors, filmstrip projectors, and ditto machines. While the laminating machine can trace its origins back to Barrow, famous for his efforts in book-making and document restoration, it did not find popular use until the 1970s. The old tried-and-true overhead projector came on the scene in the 1960s, brainchild of 3M's Roger Appledom. In most schools, this equipment was maintained and housed in the school library, under the direction of the librarian. Some large schools even employed additional librarians to be in charge of equipment. However, when computers came on the scene, the need increased for knowledgeable educators to help with the new devices.

The position of technology specialist first came into being in the early to mid-1980s. Dr. David Moursund wrote a book in 1985 called *The Computer Coordinator* in which he described this new job description that he predicted would be offered more and more in the future from that date. When he revised the book in 1995, he changed the title to *The Technology Coordinator*. Moursund's stated reason was that the position's responsibilities had increased to the point that a broader title was needed. Once the position of "computer coordinator/technology coordinator/specialist/director/teacher" was created, the numbers of people entering into this field grew exponentially, and duties regarding computer management as well as instruction began to split. The names for people working with technology in schools are legion. In this book, we will use technology specialist and the informal appellation of "techhead" most commonly.

Librarians

Of course librarianship is not a new profession. In schools, librarians have a long and proud history of serving all patrons in their environments. As technology increased in importance, forward-looking librarians were quick to embrace the growing wealth of resources. Regarding hardware, prior to computers, librarians were usually in charge of acquiring, circulating, and managing equipment such as projectors, sound devices, and so on. The expectation that they continue in this vein was a given in many schools. At inventory time, the list of items to record became longer and longer. While some schools were quick to hire technology specialists, many others relied on librarians to become experts in the use as well as oversight of computers. Then when techheads were brought on board, it was sometimes hard to delineate the duties of the two positions. Unfortunately, in some cases, this led to turf wars and other power struggles. Since technology brings more than enough work for all involved in promoting use and managing equipment, collaboration is far preferable to competition . . . hence the decision to write this book.

GUI—A Real Game Changer

Those who came into education later than the 1990s may not remember, but GUI (graphical user interface) was a very dramatic development. It radically changed how people interacted with computers. Users were freed from keyboard commands and instead were able to use that lovable new rodent on the block, the mouse (Figure 1.4). While the concept goes all the way back to the 1970s, actual use did not flourish until the late 1980s. Then, all of a sudden, those who were into computing began talking about GUI this and GUI that, further

Figure 1.4: GUI (graphical user interface) brought about the need for the computer mouse.

frustrating the Luddites still trying to hold out against computer use. The new point-and-click technology caused old operating systems to stagger along and fail. And then came Windows, Microsoft's first iteration came into being in 1985, and meanwhile Apple was touting Lisa and then new computers called Macintosh. Along the way, and equally exciting for users, color came on the screen scene with the first color Macintosh in 1987 (Computer History Museum). Every new development had early adopters salivating for the next.

The new OS features and other developments proved to make computers increasingly user-friendly as well as powerful. The bandwagon was getting crowded, and more schools and districts called upon technology faculty and librarians to provide staff development to help bring educators along. As has always been the case, youngsters needed little or no prompting. The truism that kids know more about many aspects of technology was accurate then and continues to be so.

Networking and Infrastructure

By the 1990s, most schools were hiring people to oversee the use of fast-emerging technology. Net Day came and went, bringing about more attention and emphasis on technology. State and national standards were drafted to codify use. Acceptable Use Policies were drafted to manage district computer use. Computer labs were still in most schools, but there was a growing demand for computers in classrooms as well. Districts and schools that were well funded touted their computer-to-student ratios. Teachers found it increasingly difficult to avoid getting on the technology bandwagon. By the late 1990s, most campuses had cut down significantly on printed or public address system announcements, expecting faculties to use email instead. In libraries, more and more research materials were available online. Subscriptions to periodical databases became essential. Districts that had wisely invested in fiber-optic infrastructure were able to move ahead while others scrambled to catch up. For a while, much information was still held and disseminated from CDs, but by the early 1990s, more and more information was available full text online. Information databases that had sent out updates via CDs to be loaded to servers now offered all-online access. A wonderful plus for this access was that students and parents could get information from home.

Web 2.0

All this connectivity was causing the world to shrink. Through the early to mid-1990s, email reigned supreme and is still vital to communication with no end in sight. But there was a growing desire to share ideas, images, and information in new ways and to communicate more and more regardless of location. It is often impossible to nail down the origin of a term, but Tim O'Reilly is credited with coining the term "Web 2.0." According to O'Reilly, he first used the term in 2003 during a conference brainstorming session. The gist of the conversation was that those web applications that survived the burst of the dot.com bubble in 2001 were robust and increasingly interactive with communication and collaboration integral features of the new kinds of applications. It did not take long for Web 2.0 applications to pop up with increasing regularity in the realm of education with "harvesting the collective intelligence" a common feature (O'Reilly).

Very early in the evolution of Web 2.0, Wikipedia emerged with its birth in 2001. Both maligned and praised, Wikipedia has become a major player in the world of information accumulation and distribution (http://en.wikipedia.org/wiki/History_of_Wikipedia). At first, there was a great deal of concern, and rightly so, about the authority of Wikipedia articles. Over the years, the authority has greatly improved, and educators have found it a useful tool along with many other resources that comprise a rich environment for student research. Today, librarians and teachers avail themselves of a plethora of resources, with subscription databases and print having particular value for students needing accurate information.

Wikipedia and other informational resources were only part of the Web 2.0 world to benefit educators. There are also many wonderful sites, most free of charge, that allow students to create products and express ideas in new and different ways. Blogs and wikis have been great communication tools both for educators and for students. Further, the many resources for sharing information have transformed the ways students can show what they have learned. VoiceThread, SlideShare, Animoto, Prezi, and many other online tools offer exciting opportunity for students to create and share their work. Alas, many educators and students are barred from using these great resources at school. Misuse of filtering software resulted in blocking an ever-growing wealth of what the Internet can offer to teachers and learners.

CIPA and Filtering

Along with the explosion of information accessible in schools came deep concerns. Undeniably, some online content was not appropriate for young users. Sharing the same space with wonderful educational websites was a plethora of less desirable sites: pornography, racist and other hate sites, violence, and general hokum. Clearly, the Internet was not an environment where children could "surf" freely without adult guidance. For the most part, technology leaders and librarians strove in the late 1990s to ensure that students' use of the Internet was constructive through close monitoring of their activities. Teachers were cautioned to allow students to explore the Internet only under their direct supervision. Unfortunately, due to the creativity of youngsters and the sometime lax supervision of their teachers, stories began to pop up of students accessing all the worst sites the Internet had to offer. News stories about examples of such lapses fueled the fears of parents, community leaders, and legislators. Thus was born the movement to restrict student access through Internet filters. Of course, the demand for filters gave rise to a host of companies offering products promising to keep students safe both at home and at school. The idea that software could do the job that adults had been performing with varying degrees of success was impossible to resist.

CIPA, the Children's Internet Protection Act, passed the U.S. Congress in 2001. After this date, schools were mandated to closely oversee student Internet access in order to avoid their accessing pornography or excessive violence. Failure to do so could result in withdrawal of government funding. The result in many schools was the wholesale filtering of a wide array of sites for a long list of reasons ranging from justified to patently ridiculous. To reiterate, CIPA does *not* call for draconian filtering. By contrast, it confines filtering to very limited categories. CIPA requires that any school that funds Internet access or their internal network connections with E-rate has to implement filters to block students' access to content that could be harmful to minors. However, this applies to *only* those sites that are obscene, pornographic, or harmful to minors. Furthermore, the rules apply to only those computers that are accessible to minors. Thus computers used only by faculty do not have to be filtered at all. The wholesale blocking of everything from TeacherTube to Amazon is actually contrary to the law rather than following it. All the same, that is the current state of affairs in far too many schools and districts.

The disparity among districts, and even schools within districts, is indicative of the confusion and lack of understanding about the value of Internet access in schools today. One school may have filters so rigidly defined that students and educators find Internet use almost a fruitless effort. Other districts have more access and the ability to unblock sites on request. A few districts have adopted the "gatekeeper" model, that of letting through most sites and only blocking those that are truly offensive or dangerous. For the purpose of discussion in this book, districts with highly restrictive filters will be referred to as "shut," those with moderate access will be said to have "middle" range of access, and those with access to a wide range of resources will be called "open." The appropriate level of access for students is often the bailiwick of technology personnel and can be a bone of contention between librarians and techheads.

2010 to Present

Computer history can no longer be measured in decades. Things move too fast for that! In many U.S. states, and in the nation as a whole, 2010 was a benchmark year. The November elections brought in a controlling majority of lawmakers in the U.S. Congress and in numerous states who were bent upon cutting funding regardless of the previously perceived sanctity of certain entities. Citizens learned of enormous budget deficits that had not been so evident in the run-up to elections. Schools and libraries were increasingly threatened financially, leading to layoffs and resource cuts. Librarians, who are often the first to be cut when money is tight, found themselves fighting for their jobs and for the future of the profession both in schools at all levels and in the public arena. Even technology specialists, only recently the darlings of school and district administrators, found their positions in jeopardy. Cuts in positions mean increases in duties for those who survive. In some districts, keeping technology specialists and librarians became an either/or proposition. Whoever was left standing was then expected to shoulder the workload of the less fortunate. Professionals in both fields now must realign their responsibilities and prove their worth. In these hard times, there is much to gain in collaborating. Districts where librarians and techheads work together to provide standards-based and creative curriculum for teachers in their schools have a much greater chance of surviving. Creating a protected kingdom from which resources are doled out at the pleasure of any entity was never a good idea and now is unconscionable. All educators must work together for the betterment of their students and seek collaborative efforts to move ahead.

What's in a Name?

In writing this book, one issue we faced involved nomenclature. The title "librarian" has a long and proud history, going back to ancient times. From the time that librarians began to be found on school campuses, the term "school librarian" had favor. In recent years, in an effort to encompass additional duties, and especially those related to technology, a number of new titles gained popularity. Technology specialists' history in schools is less lengthy, and job titles vary along with respective duties. Selecting nomenclature for both jobs, librarian and techhead, led to two surveys that polled educators about their current titles and title preferences.

Naming School Librarians

"A rose is a rose is a rose . . . " and a school librarian is a media specialist, a resource specialist, a teacher librarian, and so on. The battle over what to call librarians who work in schools is really more of a series of skirmishes that has been ongoing for 30 years or more. As information segued into formats other than print, and school librarians were called upon to manage all sorts of media, the term "librarian" seemed to fall short of being descriptive and comprehensive to some people within and outside the field. Terms seemed to pop up one after another, and many had the word "media" included in order to broaden the scope of duties. At the same time, many school librarians were and are traditionalists who believed, and who still maintain, that the definition should evolve rather than the term itself. Another factor that affected the various efforts for name-change was to come up with a title that would sound more important and perhaps bring with it a bit of increased job security. Back in 1988, with the advent of Information Power, the American Association of School Librarians (AASL) sought to settle the matter by endorsing and using the term "School Library Media Specialist." This rather cumbersome title was often abbreviated SLMS, adding another acronym to the already acronym-heavy profession. Things bumped along for 20 more years, with the name getting some traction but not achieving universal acceptance. Finally in 2010, when 21st-Century Standards came out to augment and update Information Power, AASL decided that it would be best to change the title again. Thus they studied, surveyed, discussed, and finally concluded that the best title was (drumroll) the venerable term "school librarian." After that, everybody fell into line and the matter was settled. Or was it? In an effort to see where professionals in this field currently stand, we posted an online survey that asked participants about the names they are called and their preferences as to such. I posted this query to two librarian listservs, LM_Net, or Library Media Network, and TLC, or Texas Library Connection. These two large groups provide an ample pool of respondents for surveys about school librarianship. Clearly, the survey struck a nerve, because before it closed, 573 people had par-

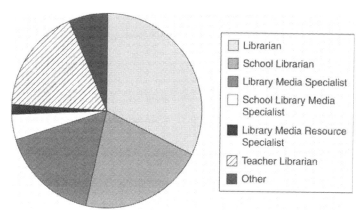

Figure 1.5: Survey results for job titles preferred by school librarians

ticipated. After basic demographic questions were posed, respondents were asked, "What is the term officially used at your place of work?" Most people were just called librarians, with the second most popular choice being "school librarian." These two options comprised 58 percent of the responses. All responses and their respective numbers are shown in the following chart (Figure 1.5).

A second question was presented to tally preferred titles by participants rather than titles that were given where they worked. Again the simple term "librarian" was the favorite, followed by "school librarian." The term that had a noticeable gain in choices in this poll was "teacher librarian." Many professionals have promoted this term to lend credence to their profession during recent and present hard times when school librarians are threatened with layoffs.

What job title do you prefer?

Librarians do feel strongly about job titles and express concern that some titles offer less information about what the job entails as do others. For the interest of continuity and with a nod to AASL, the terms used in the book will be either "school librarian" or "librarian."

Naming Techheads

If the naming of school librarians is a challenge, the quandary of correctly naming positions for professionals working with technology is a veritable quagmire. Since the positions are relatively new in schools and districts, and since job duties vary widely, there is very little similarity between titles from one district to the next, or even within single districts. The one unifying factor is that almost all titles do have the word "technology" included. Message board members of LM_Net, TLC, and EDTECH responded to a survey in which they listed titles at their schools and districts, and provided brief descriptions of duties for those positions. The results, coming from 25 contributors from several states, show little consistency other than the inclusion of the word "technology" in most titles.

From	Title	Duties
TX	Campus instructional technologist	Keeping the computers running, training for software and hardware, videoconferences, and anything else asked as well as some admin duties
TX	Campus technology coordinators	Campus teacher/staff member who does troubleshooting and escalates issues to district technology
TX	Campus technology representatives; technology integration lead teachers; technology integration specialist	CTR—responsible for campus technology like installing software, updates, keep up with district mandates; TILT—responsible for helping teachers integrate technology in lessons (not one on each campus); TIS—two or three district-wide specialists provide professional development to district and keep abreast of emerging trends and make recommendations to board
TX	Computer liaison tech	CLT—Teacher on campus who does troubleshooting for district personnel and fixes minor things
OK	Computer teacher	Teacher
CA	Digital media resources developer	Manages the server and uPortal site that deploys online academic resources such as WorldBook, CaliforniaStreaming, etc., throughout our county. Also manages Moodle site, performs upgrades, installs modules, etc. Creates content management system sites for county ed. departments, schools, and districts in our county. Assists in training on various topics. Helps organize Classroom Technology Showcase event
VA	Director of information technology	Oversees all school division technology purchases, staffing, and budgets
TN	Director of academic technology	In charge of faculty professional development, oversees student instruction and technology curriculum, research and implement programs and tools to

(Continued)

From	Title	Duties
		support the administration, students, and faculty (ex. Moodle LMS), consults with the network administrator, troubleshooting—mostly on software, +
TX	Ed tech	Find and share and teach educational technology for district (in Curriculum & Instruction department)
OK	Electronic technician	Computer/printer maintenance
Texas	Instructional technology consultant	Training teachers for technology implementation, providing technology staff development, writing and distributing monthly technology tips newsletter, trouble shooting software/hardware issues
TX	Instructional technology specialist	ITS—Primary job responsibilities include planning with teachers and assisting them with the integration of technology into their lessons; providing technology professional development; providing training on everyday responsibilities that involve technology; troubleshooting hardware and software problems and calling in tech support when needed; teaching/assisting with model lessons involving technology; creating and maintaining school website; other job responsibilities vary by campus and include sponsoring student-led broadcast news, electronic newsletter creation and distribution, professional development class creation, and attendance tracking—and more!
TX	iTech	Teaches technology to staff
OK	LMS/site tech	
AK	Managers	Contracted employees who run the tech department—ordering, installation, upgrading equipment, moving equipment, training, budget, everything!
Kentucky	School technology coordinator	Troubleshoot/enter tickets for district tech person; facilitate the use/integration of instructional technology; provide professional development as needed in building; maintain school website; maintain list of students who have signed the district's AUP; sponsor a Student Technology Leadership Program; manage passwords for all students in the building
NC	Tech facilitator	Collaborates with staff and provides instruction to students/staff

(Continued)

From	Title	Duties
Oklahoma	Technical support specialist	Campus troubleshooter
NC	Technician	Repairs, troubleshooting, website development
TX	Technician	Campus maintenance (many care for multiple campuses)
AK	Technician	School district employees who work under the directive of the managers—mostly hands-on—installation, troubleshooting, printers, etc.
TX	Technology	Odd term for everyone who is not assigned to ed tech or campus tech
TX	Technology director	Oversees all district technology and technology staff as well as technology budget
TX	Technology integration educator	TIE—Facilitating Promethean Board use in classroom; troubleshooting minor connection and network glitches; PD for teachers/staff to file own maintenance requests; annual NCLB reporting (hand counts Internet-connected devices); heads technology committee to prioritize and suggest technology purchases; reports to principal and site-based team; main contact for educational technology pyramid specialists; identifies teacher/staff needs for hardware and software; trained twice per year by ed tech dept. in district; attends and works at district ed tech conference; informs teachers about PD opportunities and incentive-based training classes offered after school and during summer; distributes catalog for PD classes and identifies teacher needs for training in specific areas. There is a stipend for this job
Ohio	Technology resource facilitator	Assisting teachers with technology implementation, teaching multimedia to students
OH	Technology resource teacher	Instructional technology coach for teachers
VA	Technology support specialist	Computer maintenance

Clearly, the job titles and the duties attached thereto are nearly as many as there are positions. The fact reflects that librarianship and technology education are in a rapid state of change as the fast-moving world of technology continues to evolve.

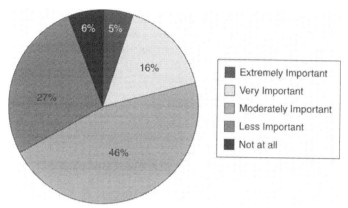

Figure 1.6: Survey results for job titles preferred by school librarians

What's in a Name Anyway?

Why does it matter what a person's job is called? What difference does it make anyway? Many people seem to think that their job titles are very important. In the survey conducted to ask librarians about this, the final question asked whether or not names were that important. The results (Figure 1.6) show that most school librarians thought the issue had at least moderate if not greater importance.

A quotation from Dr. Joanna Fountain sums up the issue of importance very nicely, "I think it is important what we call people, jobs, things . . . it expresses a value relative to other ones. I have started a book titled *Out of Circulation*, in which the non-degreed staff in a public library go on strike just to stop being called 'nonprofessionals.' Without arguing the best distinctions, the fact is that they do exist and matter. I am glad you are bringing this out; it comes up periodically, which means to me that it is an unresolved issue."

Summary

This chapter delineates a number of ways for techheads and librarians to work together and bridge gaps resulting from past and present differences. None of the suggestions are easy, and none is a panacea. Likely a determined professional will need to employ a combination of efforts and also proceed with patience. In a recent workshop, Lisa Von Drasek, Bank Street School librarian, talked about the need to keep trying to bring about change. She repeatedly used the phrase "water on rock" to emphasize the point that achieving one's goals is not likely to happen quickly. Rather such change comes about due to repeated and continuing efforts. Giving up is not an option, given the economic situation and the growing workloads of professionals from both areas.

Works Cited

Barseghian, Tina. "Straight from the DOE: Dispelling Myths about Blocked Sites." MindShift: How We Will Learn. http://mindshift.kqed.org/2011/04/straight-from-the-doe-facts-about-blocking-sites-in-schools/ (accessed March 5, 2013).

Bellis, Mary. "Optical Disk—David Gregg and the History of the Optical Disk." Inventors. http://inventors.about.com/od/ofamousinventions/a/Optical_Disk.htm (accessed March 5, 2013).

"Computer History Museum—Timeline of Computer History." Computer History Museum. http://www.computerhistory.org/timeline/?year=1987 (accessed March 5, 2013).

"The Day after Net Day." *Convergence: International Journal of Research into New Media Technologies.* http://con.sagepub.com/content/5/1/24.short (accessed March 5, 2013).

Ferguson, R. "Teachers' Perceptions of the Effectiveness of Windows on Science as a Science Curriculum Teaching Tool." *Journal of Technology and Teacher Education* 5.1 (1997): 43–53.

Fountain, J. Author interview. Email interview. May 20, 2012.

"Graphical User Interface Timeline." Nathan's Toasty Technology Page. http://toasty-tech.com/guis/guitimeline2.html (accessed March 5, 2013).

"History of Wikipedia—Wikipedia, the Free Encyclopedia." Wikipedia, the Free Encyclopedia. http://en.wikipedia.org/wiki/History_of_Wikipedia (accessed March 5, 2013).

Molnar, Andrew. "Computers in Education: A Brief History—THE Journal." *THE Journal.* http://thejournal.com/articles/1997/06/01/computers-in-education-a-brief-history.aspx (accessed March 5, 2013).

Moursund, Dave. A College Student's Guide to Computers in Education. http://pages.uoregon.edu/moursund/Books/CollegeStudent/CollegeStudent.html (accessed March 5, 2013).

Murdock, Everett. "Professor Everett Murdock." California State University, Long Beach. http://www.csulb.edu/~murdock/ (accessed March 5, 2013).

"Snail mail—Definition and More from the Free Merriam-Webster Dictionary." *Dictionary and Thesaurus—Merriam-Webster Online.* http://www.merriam-webster.com/dictionary/snail%20mail (accessed March 5, 2013).

"Video Game Cheats, Reviews, FAQs, Message Boards, and More—GameFAQs." Video Game Cheats, Reviews, FAQs, Message Boards, and More—GameFAQs. http://www.gamefaqs.com/ (accessed March 5, 2013).

Warschauer, Mark. "Warschauer: Computer-Assisted Language Learning." ICT4LT. http://www.ict4lt.org/en/warschauer.htm (accessed March 5, 2013).

"What Is Web 2.0—O'Reilly Media." O'Reilly Media—Technology Books, Tech Conferences, IT Courses, News. http://oreilly.com/pub/a/web2/archive/what-is-web-20.html?page=2 (accessed March 5, 2013).

Zafra, Arnold. "Who Invented the Overhead Projector? History of the Overhead Projector." Find Science & Technology Articles, Education Lesson Plans, Tech Tips, Computer Hardware & Software Reviews, News and More at Bright Hub. http://www.brighthub.com/computing/hardware/articles/39556.aspx (accessed March 5, 2013).

School Librarians: Working Effectively in Their Environment

KEYWORDS

school librarian, applications, collaboration, access

Introduction

In the literature, the titles "school librarian" and "library media specialist" are used interchangeably. These titles recognize the work that is completed by the person who works in the school library in collaboration with teachers, students, technology staff, parents, and all concerned others. The American Association for School Librarians (AASL) uses both titles of school librarian or school library media specialist in its literature. However, in regard to literacy, AASL states, "The position of school librarian, teacher-librarian, or library media specialist, regardless of the moniker, is synonymous with literacy" (AASL, 2011). In respect and regard to technology literacy, this chapter will feature the title "school librarian" when discussing technology, access, and learning.

The topics that are addressed in this chapter mainly concern how school librarians and teachers use technology with students for motivational learning in generating products that lead to assessment. When considering how to work effectively with what is available in a school, the discussion will include school librarians' use of technology, accessing the available technology within the school's walls, influences regarding technology's use with students, collaborative relationships among school librarians and teachers, and evaluating technology applications for student use. It is recognized that technology, both the software applications and the use of hardware devices, is ever changing. Concepts discussed in this chapter provide existing examples of technology's usability within the context of the school environment.

School Librarians' Use of Technology

In order for school librarians to be good models of how to use technology with students, they should be able to use the technology themselves. In *Empowering Learners: Guidelines for School Library Media Programs* (2009), the focus for school libraries is characterized as a place that has "fluid boundaries that is layered by diverse needs and influenced by an interactive global community" (p. 5). One may survey the landscape of school librarians to learn where they are in their technology use and whether they are working in school libraries with a focus similar to the one described in *Empowering Learners*. What may be found is that some of the best models of school librarians who use technology effectively and who are meeting diverse needs are those who have established close working relationships with their technology departments and with teachers and with students who actively use various technologies in their daily lives. Being engaged with others who are interested in and dynamically use technology creates an informative group of individuals who help to educate each other on a continuing basis. This is an ideal situation that can be replicated. Let's begin by looking at a hypothetical school librarian who is familiar with technology and take a glimpse at how he or she might use it in the school library with students.

Mrs. Francis is the hypothetical school librarian with whom we are taking a glimpse into her professional life. She is a composite of several school librarians that we have encountered or know. Mrs. Francis is similar to librarians who use technology with ease. For instance, Mrs. Francis may spend most of the day in classrooms collaborating with teachers and working with students using the whiteboard and Internet-based programs, such as TeachingBooks.net. In Mrs. Francis's library, the students are able to use the latest technology available by picking up tablet computers when they walk in the library's door to use for their online searches as they browse through the shelves and conduct inquiries. Mrs. Francis looks for ways to incorporate technology so that the students benefit by using it. Her goal is to have students familiar with engaging and practical uses of technology so that they are fluent with both the software applications and hardware platforms when they graduate and move into the productive phase of their lives.

School librarians who are similar to the one described earlier collaborate with their technology department (more about them in Chapter 3), teachers, and other librarians to facilitate student learning. Together, they plan inquires and lessons covering core subjects, literacies, skills, and themes that integrate various technologies. During inquires and lessons, the school librarians and teachers assist students with the use of the technologies. The results of students' learning are products designed to be shared with classmates, family, and other interested members of the community. The technology the school librarians and teachers select is most likely available outside of the school as well as inside the school, such as web-based applications that may be used on personal computers at school and at home. Even though recently retired in 2011, Kathy Schrock has a long list of these instructional applications for educators that may be found at her website: http://www.schrockguide.net/. There are also other educator sites that offer lists of useful applications and suggestions for their use. The applications are selected to facilitate learning. Through collaboration with teachers and the technology department, the school librarians' goal is to support students as they work individually or in group projects.

But What If They Don't Want to Use Technology?

Other school librarians, who are uncomfortable with technology, might identify with only the technology that is familiar to them. They are very good when completing other tasks that librarians do. Yet when confronted with technology, they might want to pass the project off to someone else rather than take on the project for themselves. They can even become flustered at the requirement to use a particular type of technology or when introduced to a new technological application. If possible, though, they will look for ways to maneuver around the technology so they do not have to learn to use it, even if they have to go to great lengths to do so. Thankfully, in our estimation, the numbers of these librarians are few, but they are still in schools and may usually be found in those schools that have limited technology use for students.

Librarians who are uncomfortable with technology select from the finite collection of software applications and hardware platforms provided by the district and those technologies with which they have grown to know through professional development or from continued use. They stay in their comfort zone with the technology they know. Learning a new technology application or platform can cause them stress. The applications and platforms they currently rely on and use may be excellent, but unless the technologies are readily accessible outside of the school setting, students are limited to where and when they may use these tools to work on their assignments. In addition, the ability to share their final products with family and friends is reduced as well.

Theodore Sizer, whose credentials include dean of the Harvard Graduate School of Education and headmaster of Phillips Academy in Andover, Massachusetts, as well as noted author on educational issues concerning educational reform, wrote in the Foreword to *Tales Out of the School Library: Developing Professional Dispositions* (Bush & Jones, 2010) an important piece about the dispositions school librarians should have toward technology. Sizer said:

> As for technology, there should be a variety of tools, as different ways to perceive ideas usually intrigue children—especially with engaging emerging instructional technologies. Multiple perspectives on a given topic help develop divergent critical thinkers; every school library program, through the library collection, is responsible to represent a broad approach to thinking, including varieties of viewpoints and formats. The school librarian's role includes supporting teaching, using this vast array of resources, and integrating library and information skills across the curriculum. School librarians strive to encourage students to inquire (as children do naturally before "schooling" gets hold of them!) and then to act upon that inquiry. This deliberate process respects the students as informed citizens of a democratic society. (p. xi)

Sizer, who is not a school librarian, recognized the role that a school librarian should play in the school. This role includes the use of engaging emergent instructional technologies for the purpose of critical thinking by students through the use of various resources and formats. When others outside of the library are able to clearly envision the role of the school librarian, then the school librarian should also be able to maintain or expand a similar vision. The school librarian should be a leader who is driving the vision and energy behind the dispositions related to the school librarian profession.

Dispositions are significant and should not be easily dismissed or overlooked. Bush and Jones (2010) discuss the importance of the dispositions of the school librarian as related to the qualities that students describe of the teacher that they most wanted to have in their classrooms. They conclude, "In a nutshell, exemplary teachers and high school students agree that students flourish when teachers possess the personal and professional dispositions to understand and be enthused by the subject matter they teach, can communicate and relate to students, and can create and nurturing environment" (pp. 1–2). What this means for the school librarian who possesses limited technology skills is that the school librarian may have difficulty in the area of relating to students who use technology or who expect to learn to use technology in their studies. If the subject matter is technology, then the school librarian will find obstacles to relating well with students and for teaching the subject well. Any other aspects of the content, communication, or environment that pertain to technology where the school librarian may lack expertise will cause the school librarian problems. To overcome these obstacles, the school librarian should seek professional development to strengthen areas of weakness and build on areas where a beginning foundation has been laid. Continuing education related to technology should be ongoing. General knowledge of technology dictates that the world of technology is in a state of flux and change. One should not become stagnant in learning about what's new or what has become obsolete. School librarians can and do find ways to be enthusiastic about technology as it relates to their environment. Their enthusiasm carries over to be shared by teachers and students, especially when they have support from the school district and the technology department.

Accessing Available Technologies

In situations where students are restricted to certain technologies, whether the limitations are because the students' librarian or teachers are uncomfortable using the software applications or hardware platforms or for other reasons (for example, see Chapter 1: CIPA and Filtering, p. 11), these students have reduced ability to participate in a collaborative effort with other students and teachers. The students are restricted to select from the set of technology applications that they are allowed to use when they may have knowledge and experience with more online tools. Knowing this, students could become disinterested in the assignments and their consequential learning.

Because of the importance of maintaining students' interest in their learning, school librarians should look into all of the reasons that might limit the students' use of technology and help open doors when access can be made available to them. Other possibilities that could lead to such a limiting environment for students might include established school or district policies or federal legislation. A discussion of these possibilities is included in Chapter 1: CIPA and Filtering. Besides legislation and policy restrictions, funding may place limitations on access to materials. When funding is cut, decisions are made that may result in a reduction in the number of materials made available to students and teachers. In the report, "School Libraries Count!" (AASL, 2011), collection sizes in video and audio materials experienced a decline from 2010 to 2011 (p. 8). These changes were most notable in low-poverty areas for video materials and in nonmetro schools for audio materials. Whether the decision to reduce these collections was directly related to funding or not, librarians and teachers will look for ways to fill the void that has been created. Some will turn to the Internet for additional video and audio to supplement their lessons.

Even though school librarians have no direct control over policies or the amount of money included in their budgets, school librarians can lead the way for collaborating with everyone on their campuses. They are able to represent students and teachers when sitting on various committees at the school and district levels. They can become voices for their patrons and their schools to help promote change within the schools. School librarians need to be effective leaders in the use of technology as well as the users of technology.

Influences Regarding Technology's Use with Students

While within the school, when educators may take control of how technology is negotiated, limitations may come from outside of the school and not just from legislators. Community decisions related to technology use and about how technology should be accessed may indirectly or directly influence the school's policies through opinions expressed or facts presented at school board or parent organizational meetings. In addition, family decisions may have influence as well. Family decisions determine the level of children's engagement with software applications and hardware devices in support of their children's learning in the home that then translate into how their children use the technologies in the school. By taking a look at what families determine as important for regulating technology use in the home, we may better understand students' engagement with technology in school.

Family values may dictate how parents regulate the technology use of their children in the home (Takeuchi, 2012). In *Families Matter: De-*

signing Media for a Digital Age (2011), one of the key findings in the report were that parents relied on their upbringing to help define their childrearing practices. Since the technology that exists today was not in existence when parents were children, prescribing rules for its use in the home is territory for which parents do not have prior role models to follow. They must navigate through the unknown technological territory as though it is a new frontier. They must seek out ways to incorporate the use of technology into the frame in which they have defined and hold their childrearing practices. For some parents, this is easy to accomplish, and for others, it is difficult. When other factors place constraints upon technology's use, such as economic or environmental, then parents may be temporarily relieved of the burden. An economic constraint might be one in which the family is unable to purchase the technology beneficial to the child. An environmental constraint might be one where either the use of technology is limited due to access by lack of connection to the Internet where there is no Internet service provider available in the home, or parental decisions have limited the connection to one hardware device that is monitored, or wireless capabilities are not installed in the home.

A rising concern among families and in the medical community is also affecting the regulations that parents may place on their child's use of technology. Fifty-nine percent of parents believe that technology use limits their child's physical activity (Takeuchi, 2011). Many medical news reports and even personal school playground observation reveal that children are not as slender as they once were in the good ole days when kids were reportedly more active outside of the home after school. Factors other than technology may contribute to these reports and observations. Regardless, awareness is being raised as to the importance of keeping children active rather than sedentary in addition to helping children make healthy decisions concerning many aspects of their daily lives.

So do children spend too much time with technology? Eighteen percent of parents believe that children do spend too much time with technology (Takeuchi, 2012). This is not a large percentage of parents when you consider that 82 percent of parents did not respond that too much time was spent with technology. Parents are not only acquainted with the idea that technology limits a child's physical activity, but are also aware of its importance in their child's life and believe that their child should spend time with technology. If this is the case, then how do families function? Many technological devices are used by the individual, not as a familial group.

In a survey that was administered to families by Takeuchi (2011), parents and children agreed that television, board games, and books were good things to do together. Families did prefer to read printed books over eBooks when parents were reading with their child. This is important information to consider for school librarians when serving families to support student literacy. Electronic books or eBooks have a role in the life of a reader, but as for now, eBooks may be preferred for individual reading experiences over a parent–child reading-together experience.

Families provide rules for technology use in their homes. The rules they enforce are not standardized or easily translated to the school setting. Sixty-four percent of parents enforce rules concerning technology use in the home on a case-by-case basis (Takeuchi, 2011). This may be because of the faster rate at which new media enters the market and subsequently the home environment making it harder to know how to monitor the technology. Mobility of the technological devices on which the technology is used could provide problems for parental monitoring. Also backdoor providers make it easier for children to maneuver around parental controls over technology use in the home. When children know how to use backdoor providers, they bring that knowledge with them to school.

Family rules and concerns influence community decisions regarding technology use at schools. Other influences, such as economic and environmental, also have an effect on technology use. Teacher and school librarian professional knowledge concerning technology may limit student use of technology, too.

Whatever the reasons are for the constrained setting, for the benefit of students, teachers, and school librarians, schools should look for ways to build collaboration using web-based tools rather than creating or sustaining a stifling atmosphere in using technology for learning. In order to open up the gates, those in charge of technology for the school and district will have to understand the needs of the students and teachers. School librarians are in a position to share what they know about what is needed at their schools for their students to be successful and interested in their learning. This is why we believe school librarians and technology coordinators should work together (see Chapter 3). School librarians have the opportunity to engage students and teachers in learning through the use of technology.

Working Collaboratively

When one thinks of collaboration from the standpoint of learning and the perspective of the school librarian, the first and foremost example of collaboration that comes to mind is most likely that of teachers and school librarians collaborating for student achievement. Administrators base most of their decisions upon student achievement. And this would be the example and foundation from which school librarians are able to draw from when considering collaboration with technology staff. In order to better approach such a collaborative effort, an assessment of where school librarians stand in regard to their past collaborative efforts should be conducted. Perhaps even by recalling such efforts, ideas may blossom on how to improve these efforts that will extend into the technology context. Let's begin with looking at collaboration with teachers.

Teachers hold knowledge on how to teach. Clandinin and Connelly (2004) define teacher knowledge as "knowledge that comes from experience, is learned in context, and is expressed in practice" (p. 579). If teachers have a repertoire of experiences from which to pull, then why do they need to collaborate with a school librarian? This is an important question for the school librarian profession to answer because it is one that indicates the survival of librarians' jobs and librarians' worth when rated along the lines of student achievement. Palmer (1998) addressed the idea of what teachers need to know in order to teach their subject matter. He wrote that subjects that are taught are large and very complex. Knowledge of these subjects is partial and incomplete. When teachers know what they teach is complex, they recognize that working with others to cover the subject area is worthwhile. This is an open door for collaboration. The school librarian has the opportunity to show his or her worth.

Also Palmer provides a list of virtues that may be found when educators come together in what Palmer refers to as community of truth. This community of truth is a complex, intimate group that works together in collaboration. The virtues that Palmer identifies for the community of truth will be applied here to those involved in the collaborative effort. The difference may be great between ideology and practicality, but what Palmer has to offer for community of truth may be said of the community that functions in the collaborative effort. The virtues that Palmer discusses are diversity, ambiguity, creative conflict, honesty, humility, and freedom. The virtues will be discussed here in the mindset of collaboration.

The first virtue, diversity, comes about when diverse viewpoints are brought into the collaborative effort. Second, ambiguity is included because the educators involved in the collaborative effort recognize the inadequacy of their knowledge of the subject, including all aspects related to the learning experiences involved, and the largeness of the amount of information available related to the subject and that more may be developed in the near future. The third virtue, creative conflict, is mixed up in collaborative effort because conflict corrects biases and prejudices that are encountered during the time together. The fourth virtue, honesty, is at work in the collaborative effort because to lie would betray the larger truth and destroy relationships within the collaborative team. The fifth virtue, humility, becomes the lens through which the collaboration is viewed because humility offers the only road down which those involved may travel successfully. Finally, the sixth virtue, freedom, must exist in the collaboration because "tyranny in any form can be overcome only by invoking the grace of great things" (Parker, 1998, p. 108). Great things are defined by Palmer as "the subjects around which the circle of seekers has always gathered—not the disciplines that study these subjects, not the texts that talk about them, not the theories that explain them, but the things themselves" (p. 107). Please refer to Palmer for more about "The Grace of Great Things."

In addition to the philosophy of Palmer, the school librarian profession does respond and offer support for the importance of school librarians and teachers collaborating. The American Association of School Librarians (AASL) provides a wealth of resources for school librarians. *Empowering Learners: Guidelines for School Library Programs* (AASL, 2009) is one of these sources. In this publication, guidelines are provided to help school librarians interact in a flexible learning environment. In regard to building collaborative partnerships, the guideline states, "The school library media program promotes collaboration among members of the learning community and encourages learners to be independent, lifelong users and producers of ideas and information" (p. 20). This resource goes on to explain that all members of the learning community share in empowering students "to take an active role in shaping their learning" (p. 20). In addition, the school librarian has the role of learning from students whereby he or she gathers knowledge from students and educators. This knowledge would include information about technologies that could be used more widely within the school. It would be the school librarian's job to demonstrate the technology's effective use with students in the learning environment. This is part of a collaborative relationship with teachers. It is also the school librarian modeling collaboration for educators. If school librarians are effectively collaborating with teachers and modeling the behavior, then they should be able to collaborate with technology staff as well.

AASL is such a strong supporter of collaboration that the organization offers the AASL Collaborative School Library Award of

$2,500. The award was established in 2000 and is sponsored by Highsmith. The award recognizes collaboration between school librarians and teachers who meet the goals outlined in *Empowering Learners: Guidelines for School Library Programs*. The collaborative program should support the curriculum and use school library resources. The technology staff may be a part of this collaboration because they have so much to offer in regard to what is made available to students and in the implementation of the technology within a school.

Using Available Technology Applications

Using applications found on the Internet is important. Many times, these applications are free and available anytime, anywhere one has a connection. When technology departments provide hardware devices for students and teachers to use that have Internet connectivity, then use of Internet applications can be had in the schools. If wireless technology is accessible, then application use becomes mobile and not tied to one lab or one room. If students are allowed to bring in and use their own devices (i.e., mobile technology), then the school and district do not have to fund the purchase of hardware for every student. In order for mobile technology to be used, proponents recommend that everyone follow and teach common protocol, for example, people should turn off cell phones when attending meetings, movies, ceremonies, celebrations, and other events. Also educators should be aware that many of the proponents for cell phone use in the classroom are parents who want to be able to reach their child in case of an emergency. Yet there are some schools and some facilities that have taken charge of blocking cell phone use by installing blocking devices that prevent cell phones from working. Some advocates who are against cell phone usage in the classroom believe that cell phones offer distractions for students, opportunities for cheating, and create privacy issues. Some school districts, such as New York City's public school system, prohibit students from bringing cell phones to school. Visit http://www.nyc.gov and search for "public school cell phone policy information" to learn more. The policy has been in place for more than 15 years.

Decisions regarding cell phone use in schools are usually made at the local level, such as in the case of New York City's schools. These local decisions determine the needs of the community pertaining to items such as lack of access to technology and how to best meet the identified needs. Something that must be kept in mind is that in many communities, not all students have access to cell phones. Somehow the technology hardware should be provided for students' learning. Students need to be creating using technology while they are learning for their continued growth. School librarians and teachers should collaborate using the available software applications and hardware devices for student learning.

Technology use should be purposeful and powerful for school librarians, students, and teachers. They should know how to access the technology that is available to them. Also they should know how to use the technology with students following best practices. In the past, school librarians and teachers have regretfully admitted to possessing technology but not knowing how to set it up or even how to use it if the technology was in place. Intentions were high when the technology was purchased, but somewhere along the way, the training in the technology's use was suspended or neglected. The end result was a loss in instructional or student use of the technology because it remained in storage and inaccessible. Unfortunately, situations such as these usually occurred in places where technology departments were understaffed making it very difficult for the technology staff to complete even the simplest of tasks that were set before them without working overtime to meet the needs of the school district. Yet access and knowing how to use the technology that is being provided to students, teachers, and librarians are keys for success. Recognition of what leads to success has led to a greater emphasis on staffing in technology departments. Creativity incorporated by administration has included teachers and school librarians into the mix of supporting the staffing for technology purposes as well. Many organizational designs and trials have been undertaken as workable solutions along the way. As teachers and school librarians worked with the technology department, new ways of doing education have come about for technology implementation in the schools.

One means for successful technology is to use software applications and hardware devices in collaborative projects. Collaboration using software applications is able to offer so much for students and teachers. Many students are already collaborating online when they are not in school through their social networking experiences. Educators attempt to connect with students' interests by using what students know and use in the learning process. In some cases, school librarians and their libraries have led the way with their websites, blogs, wikis, and social networking pages like Facebook, Shelfari, Good Reads, and more.

In places where access to technology applications that peak students' interest is restricted, the school librarian is able to take a leadership role through educating parents, the community, administration, faculty, and students about the benefits of using multiple applications for learning that are available online. One place to begin is with professional development for teachers and administrators. Various online sources are already in place and available for the school librarian. One source, Integrating Technology for Active Lifelong Learning provides online courses for free or for a small cost whereby educators are able to gain knowledge about tools that help with online learning in areas such as language learning, Web Quests, personal development, and courses on how to use Moodle, a free web application learning management system. A more well-known organization that supports school librarians in their role as leaders who promote technology on their school campus is the International Society for Technology in Education (ISTE) and its Media Specialists Special Interest Group. By going to http://www.iste.org, school librarians are able to locate information on professional development, a calendar of events, the ISTE standards for students, teachers, and administrators, and social networking communities to join. At the state level, school librarians are able to locate local affiliates of ISTE. These state organizations support schools and libraries. Awards are given by special interest groups of these organizations recognizing collaboration efforts and programs developed by teachers and school librarians using technology for learning with students. All of these sources and more that are available online support professional development and the use of technology in schools and libraries.

When school librarians offer professional development for teachers and administrators, the professional knowledge will grow in the educational community. Also the recognition of the need to review the technology use policy will become apparent. The school librarian will want to work with the technology committee to rewrite the policy concerning access and use so that the environment is less restrictive for teachers, administrators, and students while maintaining safety. Also the technology committee should work with teachers and school librarians who are using technology not only to ensure safety when students are accessing the online environment, but also to provide for the necessary software applications that stimulate and generate learning with students. In addition, access to these software applications helps teachers and school librarians assess when learning has taken place. The result of the technology committee, teachers, and school librarians working together toward a common goal will help reduce the limitations to student learning and technology use.

Evaluating Technology Applications

When considering the pedagogy behind the use of web-based applications and student learning and assessment, the pedagogy must be open to students following their interests and making choices, students answering their questions, and students seeing their learning produce results from the knowledge they have gained. There must be a variety of projects and products available to the students whereby they may produce evidence of learning. Technology applications are very useful for these purposes. Variety and choice of which technology applications to use for and by students can be motivational to their learning. Otherwise, predetermined, teacher-selected, and possibly limiting technology either becomes the driver of the learning rather than a tool to aid in learning, or the structure of the learning experience is dictated such that student interest is left out of the equation. Forcing a square peg into a round hole is a difficult task. In this case, the square peg would be using technology or some other structure to lead learning. The round hole would be where the student interests are the rule. Only one of the two will dominate the learning experience. The square peg of preselected technology could be forced upon the round hole of student interests. However, it would be much easier to embrace a model of learning and assessment that facilitates student interests and motivation to learn. When students have intrinsic incentive and choices over technology tools to use for their learning, they have more control over the outcome of the learning experience.

Blaming the budget and policy is an easy way to stifle the embracing of new ways of using technology. Many school librarians, teachers, and technology departments have faced tightly controlled budgets or even a lack of funding impacting hardware devices and software applications available for use. Yet incredible amounts of money have been spent on initial funding of technology for schools and for upgrades and maintenance. The amounts are even topics of political debate, at both the local and national levels. The debate arises because the general public wants a return for the money spent. What better way to show them, other than standardized test scores, than to allow students to demonstrate their learning when and where appropriate as deemed by students, teachers, school administrators, and their communities. Web-based tools provide the platform for sharing students' products as a form of assessment of their learning with the community.

For many school librarians, one example of justification for collaboration with students and teachers and sharing student products that demonstrate their learning using web-based applications can be found in book trailers as a product of students' comprehension of their reading. School librarians have the ability to display the students' work in the library by looping the trailers for patrons to view or making them available through the school library website or blog. School librarians can encourage and help students produce their own book trailers using various software applications. For example, instructions for how to create a book trailer may be found at Naomi Bates's blog site, "YA Books and More: Reviews and Digital Media of Current Young Adult Books and More" at http://naomibates.blogspot.com/2008/07/how-i-create-digital-booktrailers.html. Naomi uses Photostory or Moviemaker. Yet there are other software applications that students may find that they prefer to use to create a book trailer. The software application is the tool that students use in their learning. The result of the use of the software application provides the means for demonstrating intellectual growth. Students are able to collaborate with classroom teachers and school librarians in the creation of book trailers as well as other student products that use technology for the purpose not only of creating and generating a product, but also to show growth that is accessible and leads to assessment of knowledge and skills.

When working with teachers to decide on what kind of applications students should use for their learning, school librarians have to consider what types of applications would be best for students to use. Both teachers and school librarians will make decisions based on curricular requirements. However, other considerations should include what the application is able to do and provide for the students' experience. Cox (2009) lists five key attributes when evaluating online applications for students to use for their learning. They are:

1. Ubiquitous access
2. Authentic appearance
3. Intuitive design and function
4. Sharing among users
5. Portability

First on the list is ubiquitous access. Ubiquitous access allows for students to be creative anywhere. Students would not be restricted to the on-campus setting for conducting their learning. Their learning could happen anytime or anywhere.

Second, web-based applications that are selected for use with students should be authentic in appearance. Authenticity is reflective of what students know and of what students are expected to encounter in the real world. Requiring students to use another technology tool that lacks authenticity should have sound reasoning and buy-in from the students. Otherwise, students may lack motivation to learn using the technology placed before them. Increasing student interest in their learning should be a goal. For example, a student who is learning about science may create multimedia publications for the web using podcasts or video creation to disseminate what was learned. The applications that are used would be those that are readily accessible, such as Animoto or Stupeflix Studio.

Third, intuitive design and function means that students, teachers, and school librarians alike will not spend a great amount of time on training on how to use the tool. Rather time is better spent in the learning process and in creating using the technology application. The process of learning can be more spontaneous when using the application, eliminating the need for additional instruction on how to use the application.

Fourth, sharing among users in the learning process, usually through collaboration or by showing fellow students the results of their learning, gives students a larger audience than only their teachers who grade the work. Peer-review and feedback becomes possible. Online applications that allow parents to view their children's work, such as YouTube, School Tube, or Vimeo, make available the curriculum and what is expected of their children. Parents have the opportunity to become more active participants in their children's learning even when they have little time to attend school events, such as parent conferences, family literacy nights, or other stimulating events that are often associated with book fairs.

Fifth is portability and has been discussed previously. Learning that can be taken outside of the classroom and away from the students' desk allows for greater connections to situations that occur in the everyday lives of people that are in the community where students live. The design is not to increase the amount of homework for students, but rather to allow students to make connections that are meaningful to them or to bring that in which they are interested into the classroom that reflects the curriculum and what they are learning.

Accomplishing the successful use of applications that incorporate the five attributes that support student learning will lead school librarians to consider innovative technology. They will become people who have vision for what students can use for critical thinking and problem solving if they are not already leading the charge. They sit on technology committees and collaborate with technology staff. When considering new technology, they look for risks as well as value weighing each carefully during the decision-making process. Driving to keep the learning experience fresh and stimulating for students and delivering robust content are primary goals for the successful school librarian.

In the end, it comes down to school librarians using what they have available and advocating for what they need. Without the ability to use technology with ease and collaborating with teachers in their use of technology, school librarians will not have a seat at the table concerning technology decisions. The school library exists in a world where technology plays a major part and where students should be literate in how to use the applications available to access knowledge and generate products as a result of their learning. School librarians can lead the way to providing access to students for a stimulating learning environment using technology.

Summary

The topics that were considered in this chapter mainly concerned how school librarians and teachers use technology with students. The use of technology is to facilitate learning. Through collaboration with teachers and the technology department, the school librarians' goal is to support students in their use of software applications and hardware devices as they work individually or in group projects. Creating and maintaining access for the available technologies within the school's walls help sustain students' interest in their learning. How students use technologies at school is influenced by family values because these values are reflected in how students use software applications and hardware devices at school. Effective technology use with students is demonstrated by school librarians in the learning environment through collaborative relationships with teachers. Successful technology use includes evaluating technology applications for student use.

Works Cited

American Association of School Librarians. *Empowering Learners: Guidelines for School Library Media Programs.* Chicago: American Association of School Librarians, 2009.

American Association of School Librarians. "School Libraries Count!" National Longitudinal Survey of School Library Programs. Chicago: American Association of School Librarians, 2011.

American Library Association. "Who School Librarians Are and Learning4Life: American Association of School Librarians (AASL)." American Library

Association. http://www.ala.org/aasl/aboutaasl/aaslcommunity/quicklinks/el/ elwho (accessed March 4, 2013).

Bush, Gail, and Jones, Jami B. *Tales out of the School Library: Developing Professional Dispositions*. Santa Barbara, CA: Libraries Unlimited, 2010.

Clandinin, D.J., and Connelly, F.M. "Knowledge, Narrative and Self-Study." In *International Handbook of Self-Study of Teaching and Teacher Education Practices*, J.J. Loughran, M.L. Hamilton, V.K. LaBoskey, and T. Russell (eds.). Dordrecht, the Netherlands: Kluwer Publishers (2004): 575–600.

Cox, Ernie J. "The Collaborative Mind: Tools for 21st Century Learning." *Multimedia & Internet@Schools* 16, no. 5 (2009): 10–14.

Palmer, Parker J. *The Courage to Teach: Exploring the Inner Landscape of a Teacher's Life*. San Francisco: Jossey-Bass, 1998.

Takeuchi, Lori, M. "Families, learning, and media: an evolving ecology." Speech, American Library Association 2012 Annual Conference from American Library Association, Anaheim, CA, June 24, 2012.

Takeuchi, Lori, M. *Families Matter: Designing Media for a Digital Age*. New York: The Joan Ganz Cooney Center at Sesame Workshop, 2011.

CHAPTER 3

The Technology Department: Appraising Current Responsibilities and Challenges

---

KEYWORDS

information society, Facebook, Twitter, copyright, knowledge management, access, collaboration, communication, technology and school-age children

---

Introduction

In this chapter, we would like to explore the Technology Department within the current, always connected, always on Facebook-a-chino-land and how we and our users understand ourselves and each other. Firstly, start with a bit of history and with how users learn and become comfortable with technology will put into perspective the daily tasks of the Technology Department, whether within the library or outside of the library, and its responsibility of service to users. This service varies, not in scope, but in application as the comfort level, experience, and ability of our users vary from individual, group, or department; that is, faculty, student, or staff member; teaching department; committee or ad hoc group. Also, in this, we find the responsibility of consulting and training our users and, indeed, our own group. This is meant in general for our departments and specifically for individuals. Throughout we assert that the term "user" refers to an individual or one of these groups. It is important to treat these as such. Secondly, how we manage the local understandings of our services, projects, and training materials. Consulting and training lead to better understanding to both the Technology Department and the learners, leading to a shared vocabulary and, ultimately, better communication. Herein lie the challenges as well. With limited time and, certainly, limited budgets, we will look at a few ways that we have found to be the best ways to foster conversations, conversations that travel along different modes and lines—verbal, written, voicemail, email, chat, tweeting, and the like. In the main, it seems that most of these questions can be answered within the context of a team. This will be examined further in Chapter 6 as well. Here, in this chapter, I will outline what I call the Techheads group. The Techheads serves as a sort of clearing house for information, leadership, management, and communication across the institutions. As such, it is vital that all parties be represented without creating a group that is too large to accomplish anything truly meaningful. And this is the goal that the Technology Department, in conjunction with librarians, faculty, staff, and possibly students, assists in the leadership of driving the institution to meet the needs of users while maintaining a focus and mission of service to all.

Living in the Information Society: Universal Access

Technology is more embedded in our culture than ever before. Our users, generally, have no fear of it, particularly the younger ones who do not remember a time before the Internet, smartphones, Twitter, or Facebook. Here are three implications that we would like to mention as a context for the technologists:

- Our users have the keys
- Are we the info cops?
- The threat of obsolescence

Alvin Toffler heralded the arrival of an information society in his seminal work, *Future Shock* (1970). At the time, it was already clear that postindustrial culture had been transformed by all-pervasive information technologies such as audio and video broadcasting, computers, telecommunications, and global networking utilizing a very early version of the Internet, ARPANET. These media exerted a major impact on the policies, attitudes, and lifestyles in the workplace, in schools and other institutions, and at home. This has continually and exponentially evolved to home computers, everywhere Internet access, and a more recent growth of school-age children carrying cell phones or smart-phones that allow Internet access, Twitter, Facebook, and text ca-pabilities. According to the Pew Research Center, 75 percent of 12–17-year-olds now own cell phones, and of these, 88 percent are text-messagers. Implication 1: for the technology department, whether within or outside of the library, we need to be able address our re-sponsibilities with the understanding that *we no longer hold all of the keys*—whether to access to the technology boxes themselves or the in-formation and content that resides here.

Likewise, the rise and rapid evolution of new technologies have placed unprecedented demands on societal constructs that we and our library colleagues deal with on a daily basis—such as copyright, fair use, and the concept of intellectual property. The introduction of the home video cassette recorder in the late 1970s led to fears on the part of media companies that unchecked copying and distribution of content would result in considerable loss of potential profits. It is ironic that the same media companies continue to make and remake huge amounts of money off of the redistribution of movies each time a new format is developed. How many have purchased Disney's *The Little Mermaid* on VHS, DVD, and Blu-ray? Implication 2: as technologists we, in some instances and depending on local policies, become the local copyright cops in ensuring that the technology that we are granting access to is not used in some illegal way.

While there are limits to the power of technology—creativity and ra-tional thinking skills remain more important than ever in the 21st cen-tury—few would argue that satellites, cell phones, iPods, and the like have altered relationships and blurred, skewed, or removed boundaries in both time and space. The Internet alone has empowered the user to visit any locale or time zone merely by changing the URL address in a browser. The medium has also liberated the individual by making available hitherto unprecedented amounts of information. As the need for international cooperation regarding the use of technology has in-creased, government agencies as well as other organizations are being forced to rethink their roles or run the risk of becoming obsolete. This is just an elaborate way to state that our clients—non-technologists, library patrons, and technology users—have the same tools we have, have access to the same information we have, and are able to create products in the same manner we do. Implication 3: what do we offer to ensure that our services do not become obsolete? Keep these three implications in mind as we focus a bit on knowledge management. Our answers lie in education and the team. These will come together.

Focusing on Knowledge Management and Education

As an institution attempts to transform itself into a technology-based institution, and as knowledge management becomes more vital to that institution, information technology and its infrastructure can provide relevant, timely, and accurate information, from a centralized place, to anyone who needs it (Rastogi, 2000). One of the key universal problems in this, however, is keeping up with changes: changes in utilization, changes in policy, and changes in the technology itself at a very rapid pace.

How do we think about what we are implementing while our implementation may, itself, change during its course?

In reviewing the literature, pages have been written on the definition of knowledge management. While the definitions are legion, knowledge management may be defined as a systematic and integrative process of coordinating institution-wide activities of acquiring, creating, storing, sharing, diffusing, developing, and deploying information by individuals and groups toward institutional goals and the ability to utilize data within the constructs of a situation within these goals (Rastogi, 2000).

Technologists and technology groups are typically those who are tasked with developing strategies to talk about how to keep track of what we know and what we think we know. We are also called upon to capture this knowledge and figure out a way to share with everyone within and outside of our institution. We think that the best way in thinking about the development of a knowledge management infrastructure, the greatest component in assessment, planning and purchasing, instruction, and implementation of information technology is education. We have personally used and often recommend to others in using the five steps from Novice to Expert developed in Dreyfus and Dreyfus's *Mind over Machine* (1986), to talk about skill levels, which gives us a model in educating users throughout this process.

Through the first stage, the novice discovers various objective facts relevant to the skill while acquiring rules for determining actions based on these facts. Situational elements are so clearly and objectively defined that they can be recognized and dealt with (treated) without any reference to the situation overall. Dreyfus and Dreyfus call these elements "context-free." Rules are applied to these elements regardless of what else is happening. The novice is eager to do well. However, because of the lack of a coherent overall sense of the task, performance is judged on how well the learned rules are followed.

The advanced beginner's performance improves after, as a novice, considerable experience with real situations. Through this experience of "context-free" and concrete situations with meaningful elements, the advanced beginner recognizes said elements when they are present.

With more experience, recognizable, real-world, context-free, and situational elements become overwhelming and a sense of what is important is missing. In dealing with these problems, people are taught to adopt a hierarchical procedure of decision-making. The competent performer, by choosing a plan to organize the situation and examining the small set of factors of that plan, can simplify and improve performance.

The proficient performer is deeply involved in tasks and experiences them from a specific perspective because of recent events and, thus, makes conscious choices of both goals and decisions after reflecting upon the various alternatives to the situation. Because of the performer's experience, certain features of the situation will stand out as salient while others recede to the background and are ignored. This just happens because the proficient performer has experienced similar situations in the past and memories trigger plans similar to what has worked in the past. This is an intuitive ability to use patterns without decomposing them into component features.

An expert typically knows what to do, in a situation, based on mature and practiced understanding. When the expert is deeply immersed in a situation, problems are not as detached. The expert does not worry about the future and generate plans on how to deal with these problems. Rather, the skill has become so much a part of the expert that there is no need to be more aware of it than his or her own selves.

Dreyfus and Dreyfus hold that someone at a particular stage of skill acquisition can always imitate the thought processes characteristic of a higher stage, but will lack performance without practice and concrete experience (Dreyfus and Dreyfus, 1986). This is what we need to look for throughout each phase.

Education of Users

The greatest effort needs to be in the education of the users while training in step-by-step use within the context of a plan or project. The more the users think about the use of the technology as a tool to answer the question of a plan or project, the greater chance for success at each phase. In this respect, as the implementation progresses and possibly changes, users are able to learn and adjust because the project and *the content is the thing*. Let us return, briefly, to our three implications in light of Dreyfus and Dreyfus:

- Our users have the keys
- Are we the info cops?
- The threat of obsolescence

All of these implications vary in some form or other according to where the user falls at one of the particular stages. What we mean is this: our users have the keys, but only so far as their understanding allows them to drive. Also, we might be the cops intentionally or unintentionally as the user graduates to each phase and depending on maturity. Finally, our obsolescence might be addressed not by how much more we know or have understanding of a technology or technology application, but in our service and collegiality—more on this in Chapter 6. We will write here, though, that this is a great opportunity to work with all users in all phases. We might work it as the librarian would at the reference desk.

In assessment, planning, and consulting, it is important to begin where people are. That is, discover where the skills and comfort levels lie. We must determine how the planners and administrators fit into the five levels. Similar to this is the discovery of what it is they really want and if they understand what that is. It is here where we can take a page from our librarian colleagues and use their "reference interview," which becomes a very handy tool. William Katz, author of *Introduction to Reference Work* (1997), asserts that the reference interview has several objectives: (1) find out how much data the users need; (2) formulate a search strategy; and (3) evaluate the information. Using this tool, with these objectives, assists in getting into the heart of how the institution, technologists, and librarians see themselves handling knowledge management now and in the future. This assists in answering not only individual queries, but also departmental objectives and cross-departmental projects. This process will also aid in the consultation in answering the questions of how the institution plans on utilizing the technology before it is purchased, if the technology is upgradeable and expandable, as with any project, using the right tool for the right job. Do not use a torque wrench when a screwdriver will do. It will also answer questions of utilizing the technology for future plans.

We would like to shift more to a higher level, sort of the 50,000 ft view. On the institution level, by collecting authoritative information on, not only the technology, but also how the technology is to be used, the users' skills in thinking about the project are greatly enhanced. This is an important step in the implementation of the Dreyfus and Dreyfus model. Those involved begin thinking of the technology and its utilization in context-free situations, while recognizing meaningful elements of application, toward a greater competence. This calls for across-the-institution communication and collaboration. Clients' technology vocabularies run the spectrum. It is our goal in working with our users to maintain a mutually understood vocabulary. This begins with a conversation and includes an agreed-upon assessment—you must ask the question, what is it that we would like to do? Let's start by building a team.

Communicating and Collaborating: The Techheads

First you need a project. There needs to be a common objective to give focus to any type of collaboration; otherwise, it will be too easy to get lost in the doing of putting together a team, rather than responding to the need. This project could be anything from updating the operation system in a computer lab to implementing Internet-based two-way audio/video for classrooms and conferencing. While a simpler project in the beginning will make it easier to build a team, you want to have something in the end to show for your work.

Next you need a "brand" for your project. We really do mean a brand like McDonald's or Cadillac. What does "you deserve a break today" mean to you? A cheeseburger sounds pretty good right now, right? The brand communicates the identity. A successful brand generates loyalty. A brand distinguishes from others. One that we have used in the past with great success was our campus's Multi-media Circus. Starting several years ago and offered once a year for a few years, we held our Multi-media Circus. This was a group effort by my own Techheads group to highlight in one place, at one time all the cool technology we were using on campus. We had two-way interactive video, fun things to do on a smartphone, 3D projection, and the like. The circus was set up like an electronic poster session where participants could try out the technology and have a conversation with the Techhead who brought it. It was our opportunity to answer the "so what?" Our Multimedia Circus brand answered the "so what" question to users who may not have had tangible contact with the technology. We were able to give them real-life examples on how these worked and what impact it may have on them and their daily tasks. It was interesting to see that some of the participants came up with uses that we had not thought of. This is what collaboration does. You need to answer the "so what"? We were just asked the other day about when we might have another circus. The branding and "so what" of upgrading your operation system might not be as glamorous as building a mobile conferencing system, but we have found it to work.

Encouraging User Buy-In

Once the project has gotten underway, it is vital to the project to find those who want to utilize the technology and are sold on the idea. We would like to spend a bit of time on this as this is an imperative step as selling the idea of use to others who are not directly involved with the planning stages. We think that discussion of a model will help us frame our thoughts in inviting members across your institution or department. These folks, no matter what the skill level, understand the implications, good and bad, and are brilliant at seeing functionality that the technicians might have overlooked. This is what Roger Wyatt has termed as "thoughtware":

> All digital technologies are composed of three components: hardware, software, and thoughtware. All components must be present and operating in order for a digital system to work. Thoughtware is the array of techniques, attitudes, conceptual frameworks, and methods of approach that one brings to a project. It's what makes the other stuff work. They're your basic chops and moves. And the reasoning behind them. (Wyatt, 1998)

In dealing with personnel who are ready to embrace the project, the development of collaborative relationships fosters ideas and greater success in finding current opportunities for information sharing.

In Marshall McLuhan's *Gutenberg Galaxy* (1962), this new technology brings us back to a tribal society. While McLuhan is referring to new technologies such as telephone and television, this can also be applied to Facebook, Twitter, and other technology tools used locally within an institution. As this technology evolves, more devices offer increased capacity across formats, media, and capabilities. Roger Wyatt's Technology Quintet illustrates that the individual technology applications of video, audio, computers, mass storage, and telecommunications interact across applications toward virtually complete convergence. See Figure 3.1.

Electronics manufacturers vie for customers with their "one device does it all" designs—remember the students with their cell phones—are we prepared for this? For the tribal society, this allows multidimensional, multi-sensual, and dynamic access to any media or electronic interaction to anyone, anywhere, anytime: from the smallest Internet broadcasters to mega-conglomerate media companies. McLuhan would continue that electronic discoveries have recreated a sense that all of humanity resides in a single theoretical living space where compartmentalizing individual human potential no longer makes sense, though we are all unwilling to give up our individual identities. Because of this, in the new tribal society, the tribe is not necessarily bound by family relations or geography. Tribes are self-selective. For example, one of us is a member of an online music group that likes to share ideas about collecting and studying pre-1970s' vintage guitars. You might not be interested in being a member of this tribe. However, we are also a member of an online tribe that likes to research how faculty members use technology in the classroom; this may be a tribe that you would like to be a member of.

The online forum represents another new type of tribe. An online forum is an electronic space that members sign up for or are invited to participate in. There are as many forums as there are interests: from musical instruments to medical care to hobbies and sports to news and science. These forums may be authoritatively exchanged with field

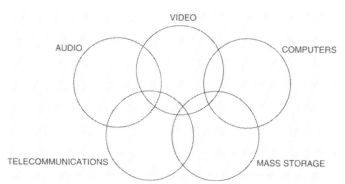

Figure 3.1: Technology Quintet, where each group converges to complete or almost complete overlap.

experts or informal discussions of what aired on television the evening before. An online forum will list current topics that are linked to the actual discussion lists. These are then subdivided into lists of posts that individuals have written either as a new conversation or as a response to another post. In these tribes, questions are asked and answered, information and stories are shared, and advice is sought.

One of the most popular online communities (or social networking website) is Facebook, which advertises itself as a place to meet people from your area in the country and keep in touch. Members of Facebook upload personal information and interests, photos, videos, and the like. This indicates that a tribe can be a small entity or a "global village."

Globalization

Globalization, through technology, blurs all geographic, ideological, cultural, and societal boundaries. The consumers are the producers (remember they have the keys). While a tribal village, humanity's economy had been based on a transient nomad system that had evolved into an agrarian system. In this economy, the village member who had the best tools had better luck taming the land: most notably, a better crop, more options in bartering, and so on. This is the case with understanding technology within an organization. Departments, or individuals, are often uber-specialized, and with that comes an aura of mysticism—the gurus who hold the magic knowledge may not bless us with assistance or guidance. However, technology is also the great equalizer in this dichotomy. As we see with Facebook and others, almost all of those we interact with have access to the same tools we have, though perhaps with varying levels of competence as we have seen earlier. How do we bring these groups or individuals together? Who is in your tribe? Your tribe should be the Techheads group.

Next, create a knowledge management system. Libraries have long been knowledge managers whether they are given this title or not. Too, libraries can, at least, foster this tool to ensure that data, information, and knowledge are shared institutionally. This can start out relatively simple such as a shared drive on your local network or external hard drive or USB flash drive. The key is to title your documents in a way that is easy to sort and easy to find. For example, if we were to use a video lecture, we would title it year day month teacher class topic: 120313vanroekelhis233battleofshiloh. Check with your librarian colleagues for assistance. You might also look at web-based solutions such as Dropbox.com or box.net for storage solutions. We really like Evernote.com. This is a collection of your online notebooks that you can place just about any type of file into. As an example of how we use this, we have several notebooks, one for each project. Recently, during a building project on campus, colleagues used Evernote notebooks to keep emails, pdfs of floor plans, scanned handwritten notes, quotes, and the like—all related to the project. Whether using a laptop, iPad, smartphone, or so on, documents can pull these up at any time to refer to. This is great in meetings. There had been instances when there was a need to connect the laptop to a projector to view these documents in a meeting. This was very handy. The version most use is free. This also an example of the types of training you will need to administer to your group and others. It does not matter which tool you use as long as it works for you. You might already have what you need with your library's online catalog.

Another good collaboration is in the administering of educational meetings or workshops where the group can show attendees the fruits of the collaborations. Whatever the endeavor, it is vital that all in the Techheads group have a seat at the table. It is this kind of collaboration that fostered the original IBM PC.

While the IBM PC was not the first PC or even the first mass-market PC, it is an example of a sea change in thinking and how a small group was able to literally change the market and continue to influence the industry today. In 1980, an engineer by the name of Bill Lowe and his team, self-called, "the Dirty Dozen," met in Boca Raton, Florida, to discuss an entry-level computer system that corporate customers would be interested in for home use. While surveying the market, resellers told the team that they would be happy to sell Big Blue's personal computer, but thought that these would not sell if the computers were built and marketed as "big iron," a term the industry used to describe IBM's mainframes. After meeting with IBM execs and given a year to come up with a plausible solution, the team determined that it was of the utmost importance to build a highly reliable architecture in an easy-to-manufacture device. More importantly, the team realized the necessity of creating an open-architecture environment that would allow other companies to create software for the machines (previously, the systems and software were proprietary). In fact, it was this road map that made the likes of Bill Gates et al. billionaires. IBM's Project Chess and its Acorn device (the PC) was a major success. Had the team continued to design without outside input and in the same way they always had, another company would have found the giant success.

In fostering this kind of collaborative relationship and information sharing with smaller projects, preparing the institution for greater knowledge management potential becomes easier. Skills, comfort level, and insight improve after considerable experience with these situations (Dreyfus, 1986).

Training

Once the project, plan, or system has been put in place, formal training begins. This is the time to call upon colleagues who have been through the previous stages. Because of their investment into the project, they are now departmental liaisons. Training at this stage becomes easier with their help because it can be done at the smaller departmental level, focusing on the needs of the smaller group. This also gives the department a local person to go to in the case of problems or in the need to update information. The departmental liaisons also know the dynamics within their department, such as where people are based on the Dreyfus model. They can give the administrators an insight into the types of questions that will be asked of the project as well.

Techno-training of our colleagues means the demystifying of our tools. We should outfit a sandbox in which clients are allowed to freely play without fear or concern of "messing up" the technology. Let them bring their own ideas and projects. Allowing clients to work on their own materials while learning the technology puts the effort into their understanding, with their criteria, and they have a useable finished product at the end. The technologist becomes the guide, the mentor, along the path of this learning. I have seen it many times. This becomes a fruitful relationship that will benefit both groups. Chapter 6 discusses this in greater detail.

Meetings

By creating your Techheads group, individuals from each department or area within a department bring issues, ideas, and solutions to the group. Once you have a project in place, I might suggest a monthly or bimonthly meeting where the Techheads meet in a neutral space with agenda items shared beforehand. Additionally, the Techheads may look to work with another off-site group toward a grant project, or the like, where all of the players have a responsibility and all of the players have a reward upon award of the project.

Keep everything that comes from the Techheads meetings, projects, content, and the like. From this, if you have not already, you should create a knowledge management system—or library. These materials may be referred to at any time. This also comes in handy at the reporting time of year. Also, you will find that this content can be repurposed for other projects as you continue to build relationships and the system.

In all phases, but this one particularly, it is important to emphasize that the basic truth of technology is not whether it will fail, but when. It is important to communicate to the students that the technology will be molded to fit the content, not the content to the technology, as the content is the most important and those involved are the content creators. Following this, students must also be the instructors in determining what the content should be. This, again, falls under sharing information and testing the mechanism in which the content will be delivered. The technology is, and should be, dynamic, much like the content it contains.

Summary

In order to deal with current and emerging responsibilities and challenges, it is important for the Technology Department to offer consulting and training while fostering collaboration with other departments, and especially with the library—though sometimes this is the same person. The involvement of others in preparing an institution for the utilization of an information technology-based knowledge management system, education is the key component in each step of the process. Firstly, getting users to think about the process, the system, and the way the system will be used well before and during the planning stages will assure greater and better utilization after the system is in place. Secondly, though just as important in the development of a Techheads groups is to help guide, direct, and manage technology goals and projects. It is not necessary, and sometimes important, that not everyone on Techheads is a Dreyfus and Dreyfus Phase 5 participant. Start this way:

1) Find a project, communicate and explain branding: what's your "so what"

2) Find interested participants, who's your tribe: communicate scope and charge

3) Assess and make the plan: communicate milestones and findings, use your liaisons

4) Implement or train based on results

5) Repeat

Works Cited

Bell, Mary Ann, Bobby Ezell, and James L. Roekel. *Cybersins and Digital Good Deeds: A Book about Technology and Ethics.* New York: Haworth Press, 2007.

Blaxill, Mark, and Ralph Eckardt. *The Invisible Edge: Taking Your Strategy to the Next Level Using Intellectual Property.* New York: Portfolio, 2009.

Botstein, Leon. "High-Tech a Brave New World." *Education Digest* 66, no. 9 (2001): 11–16.

Dreyfus, Hubert L., Stuart E. Dreyfus, and Tom Athanasiou. *Mind over Machine: The Power of Human Intuition and Expertise in the Era of the Computer.* New York: Free Press, 1986.

Katz, William A. *Introduction to Reference Work.* 3rd ed. New York: McGraw-Hill, 1978.

Macluhan, Herbert Marshall. *The Gutenberg Galaxy: The Making of Typographic Man.* Toronto: University of Toronto Press, 1962.

Matthews, J. T. "The Information Revolution." *Foreign Policy* 119 (2000): 63–65.

Pew Research. "Teens, Cell Phones, and Texting." http://pewresearch.org/pubs/1572/teens-cell-phones-text-messages (2010) (accessed March 4, 2013).

Rastogi, P. N. "Knowledge Management and Intellectual Capital: The New Virtuous Reality of Competitiveness." *Human Systems Management* 19 (2000): 39–49.

Van Roekel, James. "Knowledge Management and Information Technology: Educating Users from Assessment to Implementation." *Perspectives in Higher Education Reform* 11 (2002): 10–12.

Wyatt, Roger B. "Thoughtware." Lecture, 1998.

CHAPTER 4

Students and Teachers: This Is Who It's All About!

KEYWORDS

best practices, cyberbullying, acceptable or responsible use policies, digital literacy, technological literacy, information literacy, guided inquiry

Introduction

In this chapter, best practices concerning online safety in schools is discussed. A few important reasons for why online safety has become a major issue are provided. The concerns regarding online safety are often met with an acceptable or responsible use policy (RUP) that is set in place by a school and district to guide the proper use of technology within the school during the school day. Beyond the policy, administrators' desire for educators, which includes school librarians and technology staff, is to use best practices with students when using technology. Some of the best practices are shared to help set the course for collaborative projects within the school for successful student achievement.

Conducting a Simple Search

Out of interest and concern for students, if one were to type a simple search into the Google search bar using the phrase "danger on the Internet," what would the results be? In one instance, the first link returned from the search was for WebMD. This might be intriguing for anyone who had not thought of looking at a self-help medical information site for such information. WebMD is a site that supplies information on more than mere aches and pains and other things that might make a person ill.

On the webpage related to "danger on the Internet" provided by WebMD information is shared on how to protect children from cyber-bullying and exposure to sexual predators. The article included on the webpage begins with a story about a freshman female who had an encounter with another girl who was jealous of the freshman's acquiring a certain boyfriend. The one who was jealous spammed the freshman in an attempt to get her to dump the desirable young man. The jealous girl soon arranged for other classmates to join in on the bullying. The bullying resulted in the freshman girl wanting to stop going to school.

After telling this story, WebMD acknowledges that the Internet can be a useful tool for students, but that "instant messaging, chat rooms, emails, and social networking sites can also bring trouble—from cyber-bullying to more serious Internet dangers, including exposure to sexual predators." WebMD then offers the following four tips to help protect children from the dangers of the Internet. These tips have been condensed here for this chapter's purposes.

For cyberbullying, WebMD suggests to tell children not to share their passwords, block or ban bullies when possible, delete the email account where the bully is making contact and set up a new email account while giving the new email address to only a select few, and do not respond to harassing emails. Parry Aftab, a cyberspace security and privacy lawyer and executive director of WiredSafety.org was consulted concerning this tip.

For sexual predators, parents are advised to look at social network-ing sites with their children and help them establish their privacy set-tings. Parents should guide their children in the amount of information that they should and should not post online, including photographs, such as those that have the local team logo on it, which can give away clues as to where they live. Advice is given to keep computers in a common room where parents are and for parents to be informed about instant messaging shorthand, such as LMIRL ("let's meet in real life"). If any solicitation should happen while the child is online, the child should be advised to tell their parent or another trusted adult right away. John Shehan of CyberTipline for the National Center for Missing and Exploited Children in Alexandria, Virginia, was consulted for this tip for WebMD. Shehan wants adults to report the sexual solicitation of a child to the CyberTipline and their local police so that law enforcement agencies may investigate.

Concerning pornography, WebMD acknowledges that one of the worst fears parents might have is their children being exposed to it while online. However, WebMD advises that parents need to be aware that some children go online to seek out pornography. One way to counteract exposure is to install filtering software. Both Shehan and Aftab offer that filters do not block everything, some may even block educational sites. However, the filter will keep the record if someone is viewing porn. Parents are advised to even consider using a monitoring program that filters pornography keywords in several languages so that someone typing in porn-related search terms in other languages will be blocked.

The last area that WebMD provides a tip is for damaged reputations of the victims of the misuse of digital cameras, cell phone cameras, and web cams. In fact, children may place themselves in the role of victim by posting photos they later regret. Children should be told that even though they have the ability to delete photos they post of themselves, others may have copied and posted them somewhere else. In addition, they should not let others take pictures of them that they may later wish they would never have done. The advice is that there are consequences to our actions, even if the photo seemed funny at the time.

The tips provided by WebMD may be found elsewhere. They are tips that librarians, teachers, and technology staff could share with concerned parents. One way to educate parents about online safety for their children is through a family literacy event where the focus is on technology literacy. Other venues to promote online safety in the home is through brochures, school newsletters, links provided for parents from the Parents' page on the school library website, informal conversations with parents who call or stop by the library asking questions, or any other means available that would help parents promote online safety with their children. Helping children navigate the online environment is in their best interest not only at home, but at school as well.

Librarians, teachers, and technology staff are able to work together to reinforce safe practices with students using software applications and hardware devices on the school's campus. Students should be reminded not to share their passwords with each other to protect their privacy and prevent cyberbullying. When a student is bullied, the environment should already be established as such that the student feels comfortable to let a librarian, teacher, or some other school personnel know. He or she should be reminded not to respond to harassing emails. The student should be allowed to have a new email account and password to stop the immediate bully's tactics. For social networking, the school should have a policy in place that defines the type of responsible behavior that is expected from students. The school's policy and parents' wishes as to how they want their children's photographs posted or not posted on the Internet should be discussed with students. The discussion should include the reasons as to why the policy was established, the rules it entails, what is expected of students, and what are the ramifications of not following the policy. The purpose of the discussion is not to scare students but to educate students so that they are responsible in their use of technology applications and devices at school.

Also educators should monitor students' use of software applications and hardware devices. Keeping an eye on the use of technology is as important as establishing rules for use. If students are straying from the task that has been set before them, then the possibility exists that the task may not be the best designed task for the lesson. An alternate assignment should be at hand when this occurs. This does not necessarily require a great deal of planning either. The alternate assignment might be something as simple as an oral review of the material or begin a group discussion to replace the misuse of the technology. The goal is not to take the technology away from students, but to redirect students when necessary to help them use technology applications and devices wisely, and to reevaluate situations when technology is not being used properly by students to know how to improve use in the future.

As a Result of Online Safety Concerns, What Happens at Schools?

Because of either predators' or children's online actions, parents have become active regarding the protection of their children. Some parents have made their legislators and the public aware of what has happened to their children as a result of hazardous Internet encounters. Other parents have handled these detrimental experiences quietly, often because of their children's embarrassment or of the delicate nature of the details and emotions surrounding the event. Whichever group the parents fit into, there are victims of abuse among us. Denying it is to bury one's head in the sand.

In "Youth Internet Use: Risks and Opportunities," Guan and Subrahmanyam (2009) discuss the negative and positive aspects of Internet use. They point out that not all children are as equally susceptible to certain online behaviors as others. This is an important point because often school policies are developed and implemented that treat all students as though they all behave in the same manner. In addition, the authors bring to light several benefits of Internet use for students that include motivation to learn and improve test scores.

One way that schools make known to their students, teachers, parents, and the community how the Internet and related technology is used within the schools' confines is through the Acceptable Use Policy (AUP). The AUP is a written policy that is included in the Student Handbook and may be found online at some district websites. The AUP is a way to convey to students and parents how technology may be used at school. It includes definitions of terms that are used in the policy, restrictions that are placed on the use of technology at school, and defines how technology should be used for educational purposes. A site that provides guidelines for writing an AUP is http://www.educa tionworld.com/.

The site School AUP 2.0 (http://landmark-project.com/aup20/pm wiki.php?n = Main.HomePage) is maintained by David Warlick, an educator, author of books on instructional technology and contemporary literacy, and author of the website, *Citation Machine.* At the School AUP 2.0 site, one will find many resources for developing an AUP. Resources include AUP guides, sample AUPs, cell phone policies, and more. While determining what to include in the AUP, thinking about the use and terms of the Internet in the instruction of students is beneficial. Since the AUP is intended for students to follow, considering their needs and safety as well as those of others should be a priority. Nancy Willard has been concerned about children's digital safety for years. At Embrace Civility in the Digital Age (http://www. embracecivility.org), Willard provides instructional objectives for grades 4–12. These objectives are designed to help protect the rights of everyone who uses the Internet. In addition, the objectives are designed to guide the students into understanding the difference between online socializing and using technology tools for educational purposes.

When considering students' use of the Internet and writing of the AUP, one should keep in mind the importance of students being digitally and technologically literate. The American Association of School Librarians (AASL) defines digital literacy as "the ability to find, use, analyze, and produce information using digital technology" (2009, p. 24). A definition is also provided for technological literacy that is "the ability to responsibly use appropriate technology to communicate, solve problems, and access, manage, integrate, evaluate, and create information to improve learning in all subject areas and to acquire life-long knowledge and skills in the 21st century" (p. 24). The AUP should enhance these literacies for students without encumbering students, teachers, librarians, and technology staff.

As technology use and implementation within schools continue to change, so does the language surrounding it. When adopting new ways of using technology in the classroom, schools are modifying their former views on how restrictive policies ought to be and who should be the one in charge of the technology. With the advent of Bring Your Own Technology (BYOT) or Bring Your Own Device (BYOD) to school, students are being encouraged to carry to school their privately owned technological devices, such as smart phones, tablets, and any other device that they might own that allows them to access the Inter-net. In order to conceptualize how BYOT or BYOD might occur, com-mittees that are assembled to write the policy on use of these devices are redefining the AUP and moving away from acceptable use to re-sponsible use. The language indicates the desired results from students who cart their devices to school. Students are going to be expected to use their devices responsibly. Many more responsible use policies or principles will be written.

When the Government Becomes Involved

Perhaps fear and protection have driven much of the federal legislation that specifies schools to implement policies regarding Internet safety. The legislative authorities have determined what is inappropriate on the Internet and mandated school districts to write policies to limit students' access to the unsuitable content. In addition, restrictions are to be put in place that address unlawful online activities that occur in schools. To top it off, the policies must offer protection of minors' personal information. In effect, what the policies that schools put in place do is protect students, but the policies also specify the rights and responsibilities of the Internet users in a school and define unaccept-able uses and the consequences of such use.

The legislative body of the U.S. government is not the only branch to weigh in on educational issues related to the Internet and students. While school policies are written to meet law and limit the scope of use of the Internet with the intent to protect students, the writers of the policies must be careful to not place too many restrictions on students. The U.S. Supreme Court has ruled that minors hold some First Amendment protection related to freedom of expression, for example, *Tinker v. Des Moines Independent Community School District 1969* (Chmara, 2010). Other cases have upheld the right for minors to receive ideas (see Chmara). Regardless of whether the information is coming from or going to the students, there exists First Amendment protection that must be observed.

School policies, when restricting Internet access or freedom of speech, must do so from a particular standpoint. The motivation to place restrictions upon students must come from wanting to do so because having access would be educationally inappropriate. A good site to read more about students' rights and what types of speech are protected is the Association for Supervision and Curriculum Development's First Amendment Schools at http://www.firstamendment schools.org/. At this site, information is supplied pertaining to First Amendment principles and support organizations, education groups, and advocacy groups. For teachers, librarians, and technology staff, this information can lead to further research interests regarding Supreme Court decisions or other aspects surrounding the First Amendment and what considerations should be made when constructing any school policy that might limit students' freedom.

Teaching and Learning Using Technology

The school may have policies in place and everyone in the school has acknowledged them, but that does not guarantee that the policies will be followed. What does help improve the success of the school policy compliance is dispositional behavior of the educators within the school. The educators must first acquire the dispositions contained within the policies as written. In *Tales out of the School Library: Developing Professional Dispositions*, Bush and Jones (2010) described how this may be done. They said that students acquire and exhibit dispositions after librarians have acquired and exhibited them first. If teachers, librarians, and technology staff hold and model the dispositions contained within school policies, then they may expect to see students respond in kind. Of course, this will not guarantee a 100 percent success rate, but it will move the school closer to the goal than away from it.

Knowing the parameters of what schools within a district should do toward improving dispositions and literacies helps to define the technology goals of the district. Having a vision of what is desired of technology for student learning for the district is part of establishing goals, too. The goals help determine what should also be included in school policies while meeting legislative dictates. For instance, if a district is supporting social networking as a learning tool for their students, then school policy should state that these social networking sites will be used at school only while under the supervision of a teacher (Adams, 2008). If information literacy is desired, then school policy should describe the educational purpose of it. For example, Kuhlthau, Maniotes, and Caspari, (2012) describe information literacy as

> the ability to make wise judgments about information. By daily practicing in investigating, comparing, reflecting, and discussing, students develop habits of mind and ways of thinking critically about information. Information literacy is a way of thinking rather than a set of skills. The concepts of information literacy are practical and go beyond fact finding to seek meaning for accomplishing the goal. (p. 10)

This description of information literacy is rich. The wording allows for a larger interpretation of how to implement the learning involved surrounding information literacy. Such a description might prevent a restrictive environment surrounding the learning that students should be participants in the school environment. Thus, the educational purpose for access to technology that would support information literacy should be included in the school policy.

Other statements in school policies may restrict student use of how technology is used. Writing statements clearly should make plain the expectations that have been set by the district. Once everyone understands what is expected in their use of technology applications and devices in the school setting, teaching and learning become easier to design.

School librarians have been leaders in teaching and using technology applications with students. Reviewing simply the multiple blogs, tweets on Twitter, messages on Facebook pages, and other social networking avenues maintained by school librarians reveals that they have moved forward to meet students where they are and to use the technologies that students use. While not every school librarian is fully on board in using technology applications or are ready to begin developing a model for how to work with students in the online environment, they are paying attention. Professional development opportunities offered by professional organizations, such as state library associations, list workshops that address educational technology needs of librarians. These organizations, including AASL at the national level, provide webinar training that can either supplement the face-to-face professional development that school librarians attend or replace it altogether for those who are unable to leave their campuses and travel to state or national meetings. Sometimes these workshops focus on device-driven applications. Marcoux and Loertscher (2009) explain that "when a new technology device hits the market, we begin by trying to discover its characteristics and then imagine how those characteristics could be used in teaching and learning." When attending training that focuses on the technology device or application rather than the learning, participants can leave feeling overwhelmed by the technology or inadequate for not using enough technology with students. The intention of the workshop presenters is not to create these feelings in their participants. Instead, participants should attend sessions with the mindset that asks the question of the technology: What can this technology application or device do for students and their learning? By maintaining the focus on what the technology application or device can do for learning, the participants will be able to take away a clearer idea of how to use the technology application or device with students. The more training that school librarians have and the more they use the technology applications and devices for which they have been trained will result in the more they will know how best to implement the technologies' use with students for their learning.

What about Best Practices?

School librarians who are models for best practices are able to influence teachers. Good models have been recognized in other areas as well. Teri Lesesne (2006) recognized the importance of teachers who were models of reading and literacy as being contagious. If school librarians are able to provide models for best practices of technology use with students throughout school, they have the opportunity to spread or rather share those best practices with teachers who may be very willing to adopt new and innovative ways to use technology in their classrooms. This little bit of sharing goes a long way and costs very little in terms of professional development for the entire school. What it does require is support for a community of collaboration among teachers and with the school librarian.

Many school administrators might want assurances that the technology applications and devices that school librarians are using with students follow best practices that have been researched and proven over time. Best practices like those that Robert Marzano put forward are not available for those who are using the latest technology innovations (Loertscher, 2010). David Loertscher, author of "Curriculum, the Library/Learning Commons, and Teacher-librarians: Myths and Realities in the Second Decade," wrote that "This means the best practices are based on research with young people before the major revolution in information and technology happened." Loertscher points out that much of Marzano's research was conducted prior to 2000. Other research following best practices falls into the same category. Since technology software applications and hardware devices change rapidly, it would seem that the best practices that are developed for use with technology applications and devices must take this into account.

Outdated practices, which include learning content in isolation, should be removed from the school librarian's repertoire of skills. Practices such as these are inefficient and are not effective with today's students who have grown up with more technology at their fingertips than their parents or teachers did. What must take the place of these outdated practices are new practices that use technology to impact student learning.

Loertscher (2010) recommends that when using technology, to get the most out of it and to make a difference in students' learning, teachers should start with a learning problem before selecting a technology application and device. It is the learning problem that drives the choice of the technology and not the other way around. By allowing the technology application or device to lead the learning, poor instructional design occurs. School librarians who are familiar with different types of technology applications and devices are able to collaborate with teachers in their selection of technology that is needed for the learning process. With the many types of technology applications and devices that already exist and with more on the horizon, understanding the types of technology available will help educators in their selection of the tools to use with students for successful learning experiences.

Marcoux and Loertscher (2009) define six major categories into which technology use may fall. They call this the Learning to Technology Approach. In these six categories, technology is used in different ways to achieve outcomes that promote learning. These categories are (1) efficiency, (2) motivation to learn, (3) deep understanding, (4) learning how to learn, (5) creativity and content creation, and (6) inclusion of different types of learners. In each of these categories, multiple types of technology applications may be included for use. The following descriptions of each category and the applications that might fall into the category are discussed.

In the first category of efficiency, teachers and students are able to use technology applications together for successful outcomes. Applications that are included in this group would be shared calendars, collaborative documents, presentations and wikis, RSS feeds that deliver news and other newly created content from blogs, and online search tools that assist in locating materials needed for learning. Efficiency in the use of technology applications enables teachers and students to communicate and collaborate while learning is taking place.

Second is motivation to learn. Technology that belongs to this category includes the latest and greatest technology available that interests and engages students. This technology includes applications, devices, techniques, and even project design. Cutting-edge technology must be available for this work, but the new technology may be offered along with choices for other tools that would work just as well for product creation. In addition to using these technology tools, real-world problems provide motivation for students to become engaged in their learning.

Third is deep understanding where concepts are better understood and critical and creative thinking, logic, and reflection are a result of using the technology applications. Augmented reality (thanks to gaming and cell phone technology) and other simulations of real-life scenarios or of models into how things or organisms work make available opportunities for students to view and practice making mistakes with their decisions. Students could not do this in real life because of the potential to cause harm if something should go wrong. Other types of applications include those that may be used to build collective knowledge by creating content rather than attractive presentations. Another use of applications for deep understanding would include those that would allow for students to study problems and search for answers that affect them, such as bullying or world politics. Deep understanding is when students are active in their learning, searching for answers and developing knowledge.

Fourth is learning how to learn. This incorporates the 21st-century skills. Students collaborate and use the inquiry process to make sense of the information they gather from multiple sources. Along the way, they use applications to help them learn, such as mind maps and spreadsheet charts, to help them identify knowledge that they already know, and to set the stage for new learning that they want to occur. Students are taught inquiry models to follow, so they learn how to structure their questions and searches. School librarians and teachers work together to provide credible information and instruction on how to evaluate the information that is discovered. Applications are used to turn the found knowledge into a new product that demonstrates student learning.

Fifth is creativity and content creation whereby online technology allows for students to generate and publish their original products. Products that can be published include documents on wikis or blogs, surveys on Survey Monkey, audio and text on VoiceThread, videos on YouTube, and presentations on SlideShare or Animoto. Of course, there are more applications available online than listed here.

Sixth is inclusion of different types of learners. Being online does not restrict who is able to access the applications when devices and opportunities are made available to those who require them. Assistive devices provide the help needed for those who have low vision, hearing loss, and limited mobility. Text-to-speech, web cams, and other specialized technologies can be had to meet individual needs. In addition, second-language learners who use applications, such as databases and online resources that make available languages other than English, benefit from using these applications that strengthen their reading, comprehension, and writing skills.

While the importance of using technology applications is for student learning, the students' learning must drive the selection of the technology rather than the other way around. By selecting a learning problem to solve that provides motivation for students, teachers are able to offer choices to students in the technology they may use for their learning and their product generation. School librarians who are leaders in working with technology on a school campus collaborate with teachers to support student learning as they work on the problem at hand. The technology staff of the district collaborates with the teachers and librarians to ensure that the applications and devices needed are available.

One way to begin to establish a mission where the school librarian and technology staff work in collaboration with teachers to support student achievement begins with professional development and continues through working collaboratively with groups of teachers or with individual teachers on successful inquiry projects. The school librarian must advocate for the collaborative student inquiry projects as well as for the technology that should accompany the inquiry process. Through the school librarian's advocacy, the school community will recognize his or her efforts. The professional development brings his or her advocacy efforts to fruition in the collaboration process leading to the pathway for student inquiry and student learning. The advocacy, professional development, collaboration, student inquiry, and student learning and achievement are goal oriented and become integrated as part of the learning process in the school.

At the heart of this learning process is the student. This is an easy place for an author to climb up on a soapbox and begin an oration on how much student interest should be recognized in the learning process. Let that statement suffice in stressing the importance of students' interest in what they are learning. The inquiry process allows for students to generate their own questions based on their prior background knowledge as a means for driving their knowledge-seeking behavior. When students have intrinsic motivation, they are more likely to seek information that is relevant to answer their questions and retain the information that they encounter. What they do with the information may lead to new learning in the use of technology that may be transferred to real-world learning experiences. Experiences such as this inquiry process cross subject area boundaries and incorporate multiple learning styles and disciplines allowing for students to be engaged in their learning.

Guided Inquiry

Selecting the appropriate technological applications and devices to use with best practices helps to set up the ideal learning situation for students. But that is not all that is needed. Student interest must be included. This is where Guided Inquiry becomes important to student achievement. Guided Inquiry (Kuhlthau, Maniotes, & Caspari, 2012) is a framework developed from Kuhlthau's studies from students' perspectives that included their thoughts, actions, and feelings while they were participating in major research projects (p. 17). The result of these studies produced the information search process (ISP). The ISP revealed that students progressed through the research process in six identifiable stages. The stages are initiation, selection, exploration, formulation, collection, and presentation with the end result that included assessment. Each of these stages included emotions elicited from the students regarding the process. These emotions influenced how students acted during their investigation. The feelings include uncertainty, optimism, confusion or frustration, clarity, confidence, satisfaction or disappointment, and a sense of accomplishment upon the completion of the research project. Repeated studies were conducted by Kuhlthau in which the results proved that the ISP existed not only for students, but for employees in the workplace and others who conducted research as well.

The ISP is what helped to develop the framework for Guided Inquiry. Guided Inquiry is a meaningful and relevant way of teaching content within an integrated context. The learning occurs while teachers and the school librarian work in collaboration to support students as they work through the research process. Guided Inquiry is a process that includes eight phases. These phases help students explore information. The eight phases are Open, Immerse, Explore, Identify, Gather, Create, Share, and Evaluate. See the chart for a more detailed explanation for each of the eight phases.

Each phase of Guided Inquiry is designed to move the student through the inquiry process while integrating relevant and authentic

Table 4.1: The Eight Phases of the Guided Inquiry Process (Kuhlthau, Maniotes, and Caspari, 2012)

Phases*	Description
Open	The beginning of the inquiry process where the learning goals are defined and introduced to the students. Minds should be opened, curious, and stimulated to want to learn more about the topic.
Immerse	The building of background knowledge about the topic engages students. Ways are designed for students to become immersed in the topic that leads to more exploration. Students also reflect upon what they already know about the topic, what matters to them about the topic, and what they would like to investigate further.
Explore	The exploring of ideas and reflecting on new information are when students browse various sources related to the topic.
Identify	The constructing of an inquiry question after the students have been immersed in the topic and explored it fully. Students are guided to focus and form a meaningful inquiry question during this phase.
Gather	The collecting of detailed and meaningful information from a variety of sources as students make connections for deep learning. Students are constructing their own understandings of the topic.
Create	The organizing of learning into a creative, meaningful presentation to communicate what has been learned during the inquiry. The end product should tell what was learned clearly. Also, thorough documentation should accompany the presentation.
Share	The sharing of what was learned through the inquiry process with the learning community. The Share phase provides the opportunity for students to learn content from each other.
Evaluate	The closing of the inquiry process. The learning team evaluates students' achievement of the learning goals that were set at the beginning of the process.

*This is not a linear process, but does have a clear beginning and ending.

content from the outside world into the learning. The process for Guided Inquiry is to establish a way of thinking, learning, and teaching when the teachers and school librarian work in collaboration to meet the needs of the students. The Guided Inquiry process requires rethinking learning. In itself, Guided Inquiry transforms the school environment where inquiry learning is considered a standard part of the program of study.

To become thoroughly knowledgeable and to learn more about the Guided Inquiry process, a series of books is recommended for reading. The first in the series is *Seeking Meaning: A Process Approach to Library and Information Services* (2004). This book contains a description and explanation of Kuhlthau's research on ISP. The next book in the series is *Guided Inquiry: Learning in the 21st Century* (2007). This second book is considered the foundation of the Guided Inquiry process. The content covers why Guided Inquiry is important for schools at this point in time. The last book in the series is *Guided Inquiry Design: A Framework for Inquiry in Your School* (2012). The third book is a how-to for implementation of the Guided Inquiry process.

Summary

This chapter has discussed best practices concerning online safety in schools. In addition, important reasons for why online safety has become a major issue were provided. The AUP was presented as a means for guiding the proper use of technology within the school during the school day. With the AUP in place, teachers, school librarians, and technology staff should model dispositions that they wish students to emulate and that are found in the AUP. In addition, administrators want teachers and school librarians to follow best practices with students when using technology. Some of the best practices shared include the six major categories defined by Marcoux and Loertscher (2009) for technology use and the eight phases of the Guided Inquiry process as identified by Kuhlthau, Maniotes, and Caspari (2012). These best practices were discussed to help set the course for collaborative projects within the school for successful student achievement.

Works Cited

Adams, Helen R. "Dusting Off the Acceptable Use Policy (AUP)." *School Library Media Activities Monthly* 25, no. 4 (December 2008): 56.

American Association of School Librarians. *Empowering Learners: Guidelines for School Library Media Programs.* Chicago: American Association of School Librarians, 2009.

Bush, Gail, and Jones, Jami B. *Tales out of the School Library: Developing Professional Dispositions.* Santa Barbara, CA: Libraries Unlimited, 2010.

California Technology Assistance Project 8. "Sample AUPs." Cyber Safety: Awareness, Education, and Prevention. http://www.ctap8.org/cybersafety/html/sample_aups.php#!cyber-safety/c5h (accessed March 4, 2013).

Chmara, Theresa. "Minors' First Amendment Rights: CIPA & School Libraries." *Knowledge Quest* 30, no. 1 (September/October, 2010): 17–21.

"Cybercrime.gov." Computer Crime & Intellectual Property Section, United States Department of Justice. http://www.justice.gov/criminal/cybercrime/ (accessed March 4, 2013).

"Getting Started on the Internet: Developing an Acceptable Use Policy." Education World: The Educator's Best Friend. http://www.educationworld.com/a_curr/curr093.shtml (accessed March 4, 2013).

Guan, Shu-Sha Angle, and Kaveri Subrahmanyam. "Youth Internet Use: Risks and Opportunities." *Current Opinion in Psychiatry* 22, no. 4 (2009): 351–356.

Kam, Katherine. "4 Dangers of the Internet." WebMD—Better Information. Better Health. http://www.webmd.com/parenting/features/4-dangers-internet (accessed March 4, 2013).

Kuhlthau, Carol C. *Seeking Meaning: A Process Approach to Library and Information Services.* Santa Barbara, CA: Libraries Unlimited, 2004.

Kuhlthau, Carol C., Caspari, Ann K., and Maniotes, Leslie K. *Guided Inquiry: Learning in the 21st Century.* Santa Barbara, CA: Libraries Unlimited, 2007.

Kuhlthau, Carol C., Maniotes, Leslie, K., and Caspari, Ann K. *Guided Inquiry Design: A Framework for Inquiry in Your School.* Santa Barbara, CA: Libraries Unlimited, 2012.

Lesesne, Teri, S. *Naked Reading: Uncovering What Tweens Need to Become Lifelong Readers.* Portland, ME: Stenhouse Publishers, 2006.

Loertscher, David. "Curriculum, the Library/Learning Commons, and Teacher-Librarians: Myths and Realities in the Second Decade." *Teacher Librarian* 37, no. 3 (February 2010): 8–13.

Marcoux, Elizabeth and David V. Loertscher. "Achieving Teaching and Learning Excellence with Technology." *Teacher Librarian* 37, no. 2 (2009): 14–22.

Willard, Nancy. *Embrace Civility.* http://www.embracecivility.org (accessed February 27, 2013).

CHAPTER 5

Building Bridges

Introduction

Many librarians and IT specialists are blessed with good working environments that foster collaboration and result in positive and innovative instruction. Alas, however, this is not always the case. Over the years, in many instances, there has developed an "us against them" mentality that is detrimental to good communication. Regardless of the real or imagined sources of such attitudes, somebody needs to take the first, and likely additional, steps to improve. Reasons for poor communication and collaboration include lack of understanding of roles, territorialism, and concerns about job security. In hard economic times, the fear of losing one's job to another person with related skills is hardly an unlikely possibility. Frequently the two jobs, librarian and technology specialist, get combined into one position. Ironically, though, the best way to keep both jobs viable is often to work together. What are some ways to proceed? During early 2012, members of three listservs, LM_NET (School Library Media & Network Communications), TLC (Texas Library Connection), and EDTECH, responded to a request by the authors for suggestions about this topic. Many of their wise recommendations are included in this chapter.

This chapter presents a challenge to educators, whether they are librarians or techheads, to … reach out! Perhaps an acronym will help sum up what needs to happen:

R = Respect your counterparts.

E = Educate yourself regarding the role of the individual with whom you want to build a bridge.

A = Assume responsibility as the one to reach out. Do not wait or tell yourself it will never work.

C = Communicate and collaborate!

H = Help one another to provide the very best instruction and experiences for students.

How can this be done? There are a number of actions that can help create a better working environment for colleagues regardless of their roles.

First Things First

Before taking any action, it's important to frame the problem or problems stemming from poor communicating and to consider desired goals. The nature and depth of the problems will guide the efforts to solve. If the problem is a general lack of collegiality, then friendly overtures, joint meetings, expressions of appreciation, and recognition of the challenges and contributions of all concerned may go a long way toward achieving a better working atmosphere. Often the problems confronting those who seek change are much more complex. Larry Cuban's writings on problem solving in schools offer an excellent road map for bringing about improvement in his book, *How Can I Fix It?* Identifying and framing problems are crucial first steps in bringing about change. Furthermore, the type of change desired should be considered. Cuban cites two types, incremental and fundamental. Incremental change is much easier to address. Examples include increasing staff development and acquiring new equipment. This type of change can be brought about in stages or steps, moving from simple and obvious improvements to more complex issues. Moving the teacher from the "sage on the stage" role to that of "guide by the side" is a fundamental change and is going to take a great deal of time and work. This sort of change involves major alterations in attitude as well as practice, often involving habits entrenched over years. Such change can and should be sought, but it is far from simple or quick to bring about.

Let Bygones Be Bygones

If there is a history of conflict, in the interest of progress, the time comes when people need to move on. Those seeking positive change should focus on the present and the future. This likely means that the parties seeking change have to forego personal pride and reach out to others who have in the past rebuffed such overtures. This may have to happen repeatedly. If reaching out is consistently rebuffed, the person trying to reach out should document efforts by saving emails and making note of specific dates and situations where one party or group refuses to respond in a reasonable manner. At some point, the situation may need to be taken up the school and district chain of command. Should that come to pass, thorough documentation is vital.

Get Off on the Right Foot

If a person is new to a school or district, he should establish contact and communication right from the start. This does not have to come from one side or the other. It is great if a person already serving reaches out to the new hire, but it could certainly be a good thing for the new person to make the first move in the way of an introduction and request for time to visit. Georgia's Susan Grigsby is a respected leader of school librarians in her state, and here are her comments: "When our new tech specialist arrived I invited her in to the media center for lunch so we could talk and get to know each other. I made sure she knew I was here to help her in any way she needed and how much I looked forward to working with her. That was the start of a wonderful partnership that, if I may toot my own horn, is the envy of my LMS colleagues in our county. I can't stress enough that mutual respect is essential and the LMS and Technology Support Specialists need to find common ground and play on each other's strengths." For a view from the other side, Technology Director Glen English of Tyler, Texas, recounted in an interview that he recognized from day 1 of assuming his position that working well with librarians was essential. One of the first things he did after assuming his new position was to visit every librarian in the district and talk about common goals. He is following up with continuing meetings and communications. Of course not every situation offers the chance for someone to come in brand new and have the resulting impetus to meet with and get to know all those who should be working together. However, there are other beginnings, with the start of a new school year being a good time to instigate or renew efforts to improve communication.

Offer Small Courtesies and Friendly Gestures

There is a difference between friendly communication and insincere flattery. Being nice to people can grease the wheels of progress in any institution. Small things like emails thanking people for their hard work, for efficient responses to requests, and for help with projects are *not* gratuitous. Being courteous and congenial is common sense and decency. Speaking of getting along with technology specialists, Appomattox, Virginia librarian, Paulette Anderson, offers these suggestions: "Be friendly and open and joke and smile a lot when you talk to them. Feed them when they come to your space to help. Acknowledge that they are busy and that they are helping, as in, 'I hate to interrupt your busy day, but would you have time to…?' " Having a welcoming atmosphere in your library or office is good practice in general. Making people comfortable to stop by and visit or share plans and ideas should be a goal for both librarians and technology personnel. Often it is possible to publicly acknowledge and thank colleagues who work together. Putting a "thank you" message in a school newsletter, on a website, or on an Internet site such as a blog can result in positive feelings for both the recipient and the giver of such tributes. Such niceties should not be one-time gestures but rather part of an ongoing effort to build better relationships.

Foster Mutual Respect

In order for communication to be healthy and constructive, there needs to be an atmosphere of mutual respect. This requires learning about one another's jobs and needs. Librarians and technology personnel are rarely thrown together in meetings or staff development sessions. There is a lack of basic knowledge on the part of each group regarding the duties and challenges of the other. This should change! The individuals wanting rapport should request joint staff development sessions. A Texas librarian from Boerne High School, Jeanne Pippin, put this very well:

> In improving, or even initiating, a healthy collaborative relationship between librarian and technology colleagues, I have found that the first step is to simply respect the expertise and skills specific to each area. Librarians are likely to know the students better and to have more of a working knowledge of their needs with respect to research and software applications. Campus technology experts are typically armed with a tool chest of the latest and greatest in websites, applications, downloads and teaching tools; many free and educationally based. I don't pretend to know it all because I do not have the time to stay current on everything.

Invite the technology colleagues to speak at your next librarian meeting. Organize a workshop to mutually teach/share ideas. Don't be afraid to ask for help. Both tech specialists and librarians are likely to be overburdened and pressed for time. Establishing mutual respect is invaluable.

Perhaps no one is more equipped to talk about this need for a climate of mutual respect than Doug Johnson, director of Media Information, Mankato, Minnesota. He is both a librarian and a technology director who has written and presented on this topic for years. He brings humor and common sense to the topic in his workshops and articles, especially "Librarians are from Venus," in which he compares the differences to Old West range wars that pitted cattlemen against sheepherders. He challenges both sides to be educators first, seeking to do their best to support students and teachers and rising above differences. In particular, Johnson urges all concerned to come together and formulate joint policies that are made in the spirit of bringing nothing but the best to all patrons in a school or district community. This can happen only when a given institution is ready to change and when they support such change with adequate time for planning, clerical and technical support, and staff development. Further staff that is hired should be evaluated for their "people skills" as well as their adeptness with technology. Such change is not going to take place overnight, and the best place to start is with raising awareness and promoting an agenda that values all concerned.

Take a Hard Look in the Mirror

The concerned professional should look to himself or herself and ask if problems with working relationships stem from his or her own actions. One survey respondent was quite frank in saying that she came to realize that she had health issues that were undermining her ability to be collegial at work and caring in other relationships. She sought medical treatment and medication and saw her attitude improve. But she went beyond that and took a courageous step. She made peace offerings in the form of baked goods and took them to people with whom she wanted to mend fences. By making amends and admitting past mistakes, she was able to greatly improve communication at her school. It is easy to succumb to frustration when things do not work right or when demands for service are strident and impatient. Professionals in both groups tend to be overworked, especially with support staff increasingly rare during hard times. Demonstrating grace and character by taking responsibilities can go a long way toward repairing relationships.

During her public school librarian years, this author made a point to learn as much as possible about how to do simple equipment trouble-shooting and repairs. She even went to the district technology center and got some basic one-on-one training. When problems did occur, she was able to tell the technology staff what she had already tried that did not work and often was able to fix problems independently. When she did need assistance, she was rewarded with very prompt assistance. Another librarian in the same district was known to be very forward thinking regarding technology. This person was always up-to-date with the latest applications and often delivered staff development. Unfortunately, she had little patience for delays that impeded her progress. She had a reputation for being very demanding and strident when things went wrong and she called on technology for help. The requested help would of course be forthcoming, but it is likely that she could have had better and faster results had she developed a more positive rapport with her colleagues.

Engage All Parties

Before taking any direct steps such as scheduling meetings, it is wise to seek buy-in from all those involved, starting with administrators. Any time substantive changes to modus operandi are considered on campus, the principal should be informed in advance. If an educator wants to try to bring together several parties including technology specialists, librarians, and classroom teachers, such an endeavor will have greater chance of success if the building principal is aware and supportive. Further, the principal's presence at a meeting at some point could lend gravitas to the cause. From the first step, all concerned should be addressed as educators who want only the best for their students, rather than parties representing different roles. In addition to administrators, teachers, and librarians, support staff should be included in discussions that impact their jobs. Again, recognizing the dignity and importance of all concerned is paramount.

Reach Out and Meet Face-to-Face

As with many endeavors, taking the first step is often the hardest part. This is even more the case if there is a history of ill feelings. For a new person in a position, regardless of whether it is library or technology, this is an obvious and essential first step. If things have been going along for a time without much positive communication, a friendly email requesting a personal appointment is a good first step. Online communication is great, but for mending fences, it is far better to meet face-to-face. Hopefully such a meeting could yield common ground upon which to build. Back in 1998, Neil Postman met with a group of doctoral students and shared his philosophy about bridging gaps between highly disparate factions. He said, "No matter how different you are from your advisories, there is ALWAYS common ground somewhere. Find it and start from there." He went on to say that when dealing with contrarians (and of course he was one himself), the best tactic was to find common ground. For example, educators generally all agree that they have a strong desire to help their students. Building on that, Postman said, it might be possible to discuss different ways of achieving this goal. Certainly, a listing of common concerns would be a good thing to try to develop during a first meeting between librarian and IT specialist.

If possible, having physical proximity between the two collaborators in a building is a great help. One librarian, Candace Broughton from Cattaraugus, New York, describes such an arrangement between herself and her technology specialist, whose home base is in the library. She indicated initial concern about both leaders operating out of the same space, but over time, she came to see the benefits. She and her colleague were much more likely to exchange ideas and work together since their offices were so close. Obviously, logistics are such that this kind of proximity cannot always be attained, but it does lend to working together more closely if possible.

It's true that technology offers many alternatives to face-to-face meetings. Email, websites, message boards, and other services are great for keeping people informed. But they are not replacements for direct exchange between people who are seeking to find common ground and bring about positive change. Further, such meetings should be regular and ongoing. The type of change needed in order to build a collaborative effort is not something that can be implemented in one meeting.

Take Time

Building a good relationship takes time. Having one meeting at the beginning of the year is a good start, as is working together on one joint endeavor. But truly having ongoing collaboration requires time commitment on both sides. Fort Bend, Texas, Librarian Dana Cox expressed this: "I was fortunate enough to spend the last two school years in a dynamic working partnership with our Instructional Technology Specialist. What worked for us was truly taking the time to collaborate. We started by meeting with one team of teachers, asking questions about how we could help them facilitate a project, and then dividing the work that needed to be done by our own strengths. We openly discussed these strengths and our weaknesses. We did not try to change each other. Instead, we worked on bringing out the best in each other." A sad footnote here is that Dana's colleague was eliminated at her school due to budget cuts, and she is now doing both jobs. While such a setback is not uncommon, it certainly points out the challenges many educators are currently facing.

Attend the Same Staff Developments and Conferences

One great way to bond with colleagues is to go to a conference together. Many librarians in Texas attend Texas Computer Education Association, which of course draws primarily technology specialists. Other state associations offer similar opportunities, and then there are national organizations such as International Society for Technology in Education (ISTE) conferences. Making plans to attend sessions, enjoy meals, and otherwise have time together at a conference is a great way to improve friendship between both parties. The same can be said for opportunities offered by educational resource centers, district staff developments, and other learning events. Even concurrent attending online webinars, podcasts, or online conferences can be one more thing that two colleagues can share. Marian Royal Vigil of Socorro, New Mexico, reported that her participation in ISTE events and those of New Mexico ISTE has helped her work with technology colleagues. Not only does such participation offer chances to get to know colleagues, but also they foster new ideas and planning opportunities for joint projects.

Start Small

If people from either camp have a number of things that they hope to accomplish, it is not generally a good idea to charge full steam ahead on all fronts. As previously mentioned, Larry Cuban offers incremental change as a worthy goal. With today's great Web 2.0 tools, for instance, it may be counter-constructive to demand access to a long list all at once. Opening up one or two sites after careful planning and justification can lay the groundwork for additional access. Sometimes starting out with one pilot project that involves collaboration can lead to more successes. Examples might be jointly working with students to make book trailers or teaming up with content teacher for research with the products being Web 2.0 creations. Success in one project can then lead to additional efforts.

Use Web 2.0 Technology to Everyone's Advantage

Schedules are tight for everyone. Many librarians and tech specialists serve more than one campus, and finding time for communication is likely even more difficult in hard financial times due to extra responsibilities and smaller staffs. Keeping up with one another through common meeting places such as wikis is a great idea. The person with the interest in building fences should not wait but set up such situations and then invite colleagues. One great idea was offered by Meagan Towle, school librarian at Lamoille Unified School district in Vermont:

> My biggest piece of advice is to keep lines of dialogue open. Have a collaborative folder of Google Docs open for suggestions, be sounding boards for one another, simply be there for use. As someone who came into a Tech Services Librarian position the same year that the school hired a Tech Integrationist, I was in the unique position of being able to forge a new relationship between tech and the Library Media Center. Now, we bounce ideas off of one another, attend conferences together, and are always available for helping. If he is absent, he recommends that people come to me for help. If I don't have the time to help a teacher, I call on him to give an iPad tutorial. The most important part of forging a working relationship is being available and constantly willing to give and take. He makes sure that I am aware of tech sites, seminars, etc, and I make sure he knows about what the teachers are needing help with.

Be Persistent

Repairing relationships that often have long histories does not happen overnight. If an overture is ignored or rebuffed, that is not a reason to throw up hands and declare the situation hopeless. Instead, the person seeking rapport should try other techniques to bridge the gap. These certainly can include appealing to administrators who have the authority and interest to encourage collaboration from their positions.

Look for Ways to Use Common Challenges

Perhaps it is possible to look at current hard financial times as openings for new joint projects, something that might be called the "silver lining syndrome." Stretching funds and juggling increased duties can be difficult these days, at all levels PK-20 and beyond. Touting these hard times as a compelling reason for schools and districts to make available all the wonderful Web 2.0 resources that are absolutely free. It might be a good time to talk about the fact that everybody is in the same boat and that people need to work together and support one another against the many external challenges that are occurring these days. Joining forces and working together toward mutual goals can result in better situations for all concerned.

Involve Administrator

This step has been mentioned previously but bears repeating. The ongoing process of keeping the building administrator in the loop is common sense for all staff members. It is essential to gain support of your building administrator and to go beyond that level as needed or appropriate. One Texas librarian, Amy Adams of San Antonio's Northside ISD, said that she went to her administrator about lack of time for working with technology staff who were being called upon to split time between two campuses: "I've discussed this with the principal, so next year we plan on meeting together with each team at the beginning of the year and then we can work together to incorporate literature and technology into the curriculum."

Another respondent described how she gained better Internet access and less draconian filtering. First, she said, it was important to have a sound rationale in writing, presented to the administrator, who then told the instructional technologist to unblock sites. The IT argued against it, but teachers prevailed because they had the backing of administration. It was also very helpful to invite the superintendent to professional development sessions that included Web 2.0 use in the classroom, and professional development that pointed out the great success other districts were having using tools considered controversial in that district.

When All Else Fails

There are simply times when one individual or group, despite all efforts, finds collaboration and communication not being supported by counterparts. Frankly, this complaint is one that librarians often express. Larry Cuban states that in examining problematic situations, part of the framing process is to decide whether the issue at hand is indeed a problem, or if it is actually a dilemma. A problem that is clearly identified and for which steps can be delineated can then be dealt with in a straightforward manner. In a dilemma, however, a simple solution is not going to emerge. He describes a dilemma in this manner: "Some situations are so messy and intractable that they are not problems. They are dilemmas. Dilemmas have compromises, not solutions. Dilemmas are managed, not solved." When faced with a dilemma, it sometimes helps to reframe the situation or to break it down into smaller parts, some of which can be addressed. Other tactics include moving up the hierarchy in the school and district seeking support, and enlisting parental support. Getting things right is too important to simply give up. As always, concerns should be voiced through the chain of command, starting at the campus level. Speaking out for what is best for students is too important for an educator to simply decide to "keep his/her head down" and do what is possible without addressing contentious issues. There may also be times when parental support is needed. If students and teachers are not able to use technology in pedagogically sound ways that can be documented as successful in other schools and districts, then parents can be involved to seek for their own children what students elsewhere have available in the way of access and instruction. Most parents want their students to have the tools and instruction that they need and deserve in today's rapidly evolving technological climate. Extremely problematical situations may lead you to consider changing your position entirely.

Advice from the Trenches

An extremely important resource for this chapter has been librarians and technology personnel across the country and even in other countries that took the time to respond to listserv requests for advice about how to improve working relationships between technology staff and librarians. Here are a few memorable contributions:

■ From Scott Floyd, a Texas technology specialist, says:

Build a stronger connection with the curriculum department and educate them on how many ways the librarians could benefit staff and students through technology. They will probably have to encourage the curriculum department to go to bat with them with the technology directors at some point, but that is just part of the process. Many districts now have Instructional Technology departments. They can start with them. If their district is too small for that, it offers a greater opportunity to help the technology department out. If they share with the tech director all of the things they could do and the feedback they can provide, it just might be a nice jumping off point for the relationship to build. Having said that, you will never overcome a controlling tech director without the assistance of the superintendent, and some districts just don't have that type of forward thinking leadership. I've been in 5A districts where the superintendent still felt like he had to ask the tech director permission for something to happen. Many superintendents are older and are still scared of technology. Until they find the need to grow themselves, the rest of the district will suffer.

■ Texas Librarian Amy Adams's statement shows her enthusiasm that certainly contributes to her successes:

The CIT (campus instructional technologist) and I would LOVE to collaborate (We both think we'd make a dynamic duo!), especially for research, however, the only thing holding us back is TIME. Time is even more limited since the CIT's in NISD are split between two campuses, and of course we don't have assistants in the library to cover-which in many schools means no conference/planning period. I've discussed this with the principal, so next year we plan on meeting together with each team at the beginning of the year and then we can work together to incorporate literature and technology into the curriculum.

■ Camille Suterland, Texas librarian says:

I have had the unique experience to work at two different levels as a librarian and both times I have had a positive working/friendship with my campus technology staff. I believe that many librarians and technology staff see the situation as "I must protect my job" instead of "how can we compliment one another to make each other look better?" In this age of cutbacks and reductions in force it is easy to see why people become territorial of 'their jobs," but it shouldn't ever be at the expense of a colleague.

On my campus, my technology integration specialist (TIS) is phenomenal at what she does. She has *NEVER* made me feel stupid or less than adequate for asking a question. I believe that is necessary to create a positive work environment. I also believe it is necessary to have a TIS who's willing to say to a teacher or staff member "I don't know, why don't you ask Camille. I know she's got resources that can help you better than I can." By having that sort of trust in one another we help perpetuate that feeling to our teachers and I whole heartedly believe that is what makes our campus stand out from others.

My TIS and I have open lines of communication. When she gets a new piece of equipment or hears about a new resource at a workshop or convention she tells me about it. We discuss ways teachers could utilize them and tuck it away for sometime in the future. Then when a teacher comes in and talks to either of us we can direct that teacher to the best possible assistance/resource available.

My TIS and I have each other's back. Things happen all the time and the best laid plans fall apart at a moments notice, I know that if and when that happens my TIS is there to help me trouble shoot and get me back up and running as quickly as possible and vice versa for her. I want her to always look her best and I know she feels the same way about what I do. We aren't in competition; we're on the same team, we want the same thing. I'm not doing her job, nor is she doing mine, but together we create what I think is an amazing partnership.

- From Candace Broughton, PhD, New York librarian says:

I am happy to say I feel I have a good working relationship with our CIO (Chief Instructional Officer) and our Technology Integration Specialist. I see more of the latter because he uses the Library as his home base when he is here, so we have lots of opportunities to share ideas, news, experiences, etc. I see less of the CIO because he is a very busy man but he does make time to meet me face-to-face if my emails pile up in his in-box. I do serve on the District Technology Committee, as does my elementary counterpart. What makes these relationships work? With the CIO: Active listening and knowing what I want to say before I meet with him. Good manners … always with everyone. Expressing my gratitude to the CIO and the technicians who work with him; also I provide feedback so he knows how well (or how poorly) something new is working. Keeping an open mind. And putting myself in his shoes, when he has to enforce an unpopular (or more often misunderstood) policy.

With our Technology Integration Specialist: He and I tend to have a more free-form kind of relationship. We talk about conferences, workshops we've heard about or attended or sometimes done a presentation. This person is very supportive in a teacherly (not a word, I know) kind of way. I learn too from watching him work with other teachers. He encourages and never gives others the feeling they are being judged. He is always happy to help teachers and kids.

What would I do to encourage these relationships? Try to arrange the workplace spaces so there is some proximity so that the "information specialists" can pop in to each other's offices, library when an email won't do.

- Lisa Mills, Texas librarian says:

First, I made a decision to get along with my technologist. That's it! It isn't always easy, but I made the promise to myself that I was going to go the extra distance, remember to serve my community and smile in the process. That's my job and I love it.

Second, I think it is easier if the previous librarian did not get along with the technologist—maybe because the expectations are low. I openly praise him, go to his in-services and offer any support that I can. Don't be a controlling person, accept that there are many ways to get a job done, thank him for support, and be a friend. This first day we were in the building together, I went to his office and told him how happy I was have him at our school and offered to help him anyway that I could.

We don't always see things eye-to-eye, but we work together well. He comes to my office to visit, and our principal calls us both into her office at the same time to discuss technology items. It is a good working community.

Take a Holistic View

Kathy Schrock shared her insights about this topic in an email, taking a long view: "I would strongly encourage them (parties involved) to create a three-sided teaching model that includes the librarian, technology specialist, and content specialist in the development of the curriculum. 'Library' and 'computers' are not subjects, in my opinion. They are both very important components of curriculum that both allow students to showcase knowledge as well as become proficient in all of the 21st century skill sets." She went on to say,

> I would suggest a sit-down together, and each listing the types of things they do with students, and first see the overlap. I am guessing that the librarian list, among other things, will include some type of information literacy model that is used to make sure students develop good questions, pick the appropriate resources, effective searching skills and critical evaluation of the information they find, with the addition of correctly citing the information. In addition, the librarians will talk about copyright, fair use, and Creative Commons and the respect for the intellectual property of others.
>
> The technology specialists will talk about having students pick the correct tool for the job, whether on the computer or tablet, or Web-based. They might include tools that help students gather information and collaborate in real-time as well as the creation of project-based things that culminate in a movie or presentation. This group will also include the overview of publishing material with respect to font and color and how best to communicate using technology. They will include the fact they cover cyber-safety and identify protection and proper Internet etiquette.
>
> The third part of the triangle that should be invited to the table is the content specialist (the classroom teacher). The classroom teacher should be one to drive the content of both of the other two, and work with them to development appropriate formative and summative assessments that both showcase mastery of the content as well as use of the technology and information literacy skill sets.

Such a meeting of minds could not help but be beneficial to all concerned. Kathy Schrock is absolutely right that the third side of the triangular model, the classroom teacher, must never be overlooked. The librarian and technology specialist share the responsibility of supporting classroom teachers in all their efforts and needs from immediate quick answers to staff developments to collaborative projects. And it should be added that the real raison d'être for the entire set of efforts is the students.

Summary

It is no longer acceptable to think of collaboration between librarians and techheads as a nice thing to seek but not imperative. No longer should librarians say of technology specialists, "They are just not going to change," nor vice versa. These two groups of professionals, librarians and technology specialists, need to work together today in schools more than ever before. In most cases, collaboration can be reached through reasonable efforts carried out with good will. When a dilemma arises, compromises are essential, and efforts to reach them should be carried all the way to the top of the school's or district's administrative hierarchy.

Works Cited

Adams, Amy. Interview by author. Email interview. Huntsville, TX, November 8, 2011.

Anderson, Paulette. Interview by author. Email interview. Huntsville, TX, November 8, 2011.

Broughton, Candace. Interview by author. Email interview. Huntsville, TX, November 8, 2011.

Cox, Dana. Interview by author. Email interview. Huntsville, TX, November 8, 2011.

Cuban, Larry. *How can I fix it?: Finding Solutions and Managing Dilemmas: An Educator's Road Map.* New York: Teachers College Press, 2001.

English, Glen. Interview by author. Personal interview. Austin, TX, October 29, 2011.

Floyd, Scott. Interview by author. Email interview. Huntsville, TX. November 22, 2011.

Grigsby, Susan. Interview by author. Email interview. Huntsville, TX, November 8, 2011.

Johnson, Doug. "Librarians Are from Venus." Doug Johnson Website—Welcome. http://www.doug-johnson.com/dougwri/librarians-are-from-venus.html (accessed March 5, 2013).

Mills, Lisa. Interview by author. Email interview. Huntsville, TX, November 8, 2011.

Pippin, Jeanne. Interview by author. Email interview. Huntsville, TX, November 8, 2011.

Postman, Neil. Interview by author. Email interview. New York, NY, June, 1998.

Schrock, Kathy. Interview by author. Email interview. Huntsville, TX, November 19, 2011.

Suterland, Camille. Interview by author. Email interview. Huntsville, TX. November 11, 2011.

Towle, Megan. Interview by author. Email interview. Huntsville, TX, November 8, 2011.

Vigil, Marian Royal. Interview by author. Email interview. Huntsville, TX, November 8, 2011.

C H A P T E R 6

Where Do We Go Next? Or Give the Techheads a Project

KEYWORDS

project management, collaboration, planning, leadership, assessment

Introduction

Chapter 3 discussed and recommended the development of a local Techheads group. This group, made up of interested parties across the curriculum, will foster and, possibly, direct investments in current and emerging technologies toward immersing clients in a technology-enhanced environment. These may be investments in monies, time, or both. The Techheads serves as a clearing house for technology-based projects and content design.

In this chapter, we would like to spend some time on the process of implementing a project utilizing the Techheads group. In doing so, we will be looking at the following:

- Collegiality—how do we ensure that we are playing well with others, or can technologists and librarians really get along?

- Shared planning—implementing surveys and needs assessments is a really good ground and ice-breaking exercise.

- Staff development: project-based learning—using this model to learn while we do.

- Evaluating for ongoing success—how well did the project go, and how did we do?

It is very important to use the initial project as a catalyst for the development of the Techheads group and the internal relationships of the group. By giving a single focus of project development, implementation, and evaluation, the group is less likely to flounder and disband. Secondarily, though just as important, it gives others not in the group a context in how to think about the group and help inform its mission. At the end, there is a product that will benefit, while depending on the project, a larger audience. This gives opportunities to build on the current and create new relationships.

Two forms have been placed in the appendix that can help drive these tasks. The first form is the Technology Implementation Request (Appendix E). This form may be used to help define a project. It asks the following questions to help form the proposal:

1. Describe the project.
2. Describe the audience for the project and how the need was determined.
3. How does the proposed project support the institution's mission?
4. How will the project be evaluated and what instruments will be used?
5. Will there be any outside contractual agreements and how will these be documented?
6. Present the budget for the proposed project and include how financial resources will be secured.

By completing this form, it creates a sort of narrative for the Techheads in understanding the proposal as well as for your administration. The form itself provides for signatures if this is a requirement for your institution.

The second form is the Technical Evaluation Checklist (Appendix B or C). This form should be used in the evaluation process, though you will see that this is not just at the end of the project. This form, too, may be used to help define the project, at least in keeping in mind the types of criteria that will be addressed in your evaluation. You will notice a signature line for the Techheads group. This is not meant as an additional line of bureaucracy, but rather an indicator, that the project is being supported by the group in terms of assistance, especially with those less familiar with the technology implementation. The first two criteria are especially key:

1. The content audience has been identified.

   While this is an issue for the department and school, the Techheads recommend to the project designer that this issue be addressed prior to the design as utilizing technology for the content greatly depends on the goal of the project. This will be verbally verified with the designer prior to implementation.

2. The choice of technology is driven by the content.

   That is, the technology fits the content, not the content fits the technology. The technology has been chosen because it was the best delivery method for the content and how it is being shared or utilized.

   In any project, these are the two most important questions to ask. The answers to these questions will drive your project. It may be that the answers rarely change within your institutions. This is fine. The answers help us keep our mission in mind. It helps us to answer our "so what?" from Chapter 3.

Collegiality

Speaking of our "so what?" our answers are the catalyst in fostering the relationship between librarians and technologists. These purposes hold interest to both parties—the springboard for furthering the partnership. But is collegiality more than just "plays well with others"? D. Jones, in her essay, "Plays Well with Others," indicates that hosting an environment that is conducive to working together effectively is an important first step for collegiality, by promoting trust and inclusiveness, and increasing job satisfaction and deferring competitiveness, envy, and dictatorial supervision. Of course, we do not want to be so civil that critical thinking or true disagreements are put on the shelf. We want to have discussions and work through problems. It is important to create an atmosphere and environment where this is safe while keeping the focus on the project.

Collegiality might be likened to jazz. As a jazz musician, many times ensembles that an instrumentalist, for example, plays in will improvise a piece. There might be a music chart. Other times we might just agree on a key, time signature, and progression. During these improvisations, each member contributes their own style, notes, variations on melody, and the like, all within the constructs on the agreed-upon attributes to the song. In this, too, each member has an opportunity to solo while the other musicians accompany. The focus is not on the individual or the group, but the song. Everyone enjoys a mutual satisfaction—including the audience. How often, in fact, has there been an instance at a live show where the audience had the most fun during an improvised encore—leave them wanting more? This is what we might keep in mind in working collegially. The audience, the clientele, will benefit the most.

Let's put this in the context of Techheads. From Chapter 3, you should already have this group in place—this is your tribe, your band, those with whom you are already working. As Dreyfus and Dreyfus point out, there will be different levels of comfort and understanding. This is what we want. By having different strengths and abilities, the group is able to answer questions on different levels, without being too wrapped up in the thing, whether the thing is the project or the technology. In Appendix D are examples of a real agenda and minutes from a Techheads group from a few years ago at Sam Houston State University. This document will give you an idea of how this Tech-heads group was utilized. This was a group that had a core, though had a few floating members depending on the project. The core was made up of an administrator and representative of Academic Affairs, representatives from IT, including server and telecom folks and the CIO, radio and television broadcast engineers, campus media designers, faculty designers, and representatives from the library. The core numbered 6–8 and expanded to about 15 depending on the project— there were about 20 for the Multimedia Circus previously mentioned. The core 6 was the tribe, the band. In truth, this collegiality started out as necessity. Each member needed each to address campus concerns. You may be in that boat as well. It followed from the thinking that as the group is working together in this way anyway, it might be useful to put something a little more formal together to be more proactive than reactive. There were monthly meetings at the coffee shop across the street from campus. Ideas were shared. Technologies were shared. Assistance was offered to each other. Stuff got done. This was one of the most rewarding things campus had done with the technology groups. The collegiality, the relationships, made projects easier.

Shared Spaces

As pointed out in Chapter 5, a good way to be collegial is to decide on a neutral space for meetings and work. Ideally this would be a location that no one group or department has ownership of. In this way, all of the players have the same stakes. For the local campus Techheads, meetings at the coffee shop across the street from campus. This location was comfortable, had snacks if the meetings went long, and wireless networking if there was a need to connect to something on campus. This gave a good working location free from other office distractions. It also allowed participants to be more frank with each other in discussions—there was no reason to worry about the politics of a project that freed the work on the project. If you are unable to leave your campus or area, you might designate a few revolving places to serve as Techheads areas. Holding sessions at individuals' office and work areas also gives a sense of collective ownership. Related to shared spaces, if you have funding for technology, it has been found on our campus that offering work gadgets such as iPads, Netbooks (small laptop computers), or even branded binders or planners give participants an additional interest in collaborating. These items are used for accessing materials, notes, and like. These are especially useful during shared planning and should be used in access and creation of materials for your digital library, which we will discuss in the next section.

Lastly, in defining a shared space, you may need to outfit a technology kit to use in your project, discussions, and planning. If you are planning to use multiple areas, this kit should be portable. Many institutions already have LCD projectors. These work well, but LCD TV screens work better. These can become like giant computer monitors and are more useful generally than projectors as they have a tuner. TVs are also much easier to read as they are much brighter and more contrasty than projectors. In meetings of these smaller sizes, 55" TV with VGA and HDMI inputs works perfectly. As of this writing, you can pick up a really good 55" TV for about $1,200.00. It is also recommended to mount these on a stand with wheels. We use models from Ergotron, but there are other good options from other manufacturers. Most stands also have a small shelf on which to place a laptop or other device while you are using the TV. Your iPads (two or above), with an adapter and HDMI cable, will work as well. This system, then, is easily movable between spaces.

Once your space is decided upon, there should be an initial meeting with the participants to outline the project, the general purpose, the meeting structure, and planning.

Shared Planning

To begin, the Techheads might look into surveying the clientele, libraries, and technology departments. According to Arlene Fink and Jacqueline Kosecoff, surveys may be used in planning and policy making when the needed information should come directly from people: descriptions of their values, attitudes, habits, and background characteristics. Because these library services are provided to such a diverse population, it is important to get a sense of how faculty members teach, how students learn, where staff members retrieve information, and any interaction between each set with each other and the library.

In using surveys, two delivery methods should be implemented—print and electronic. These two methods should be incorporated similar to the delivery of other materials (course content, resources, and the like). Paper-based surveys may be completed at the library or via mail.

In designing a survey form, Fink and Kosecoff state the importance of several aspects: make sure you can find the information needed and do ask for information unless you can do something with it, stating that "if you cannot get the information you need, you should find an alternative source of data, remove the topic from the survey, or wait until you can appropriately ask the question in a survey format . . . remember[ing] that the content of a survey can affect respondents' views and expectations." They continue that the length of the survey depends, not only on what you need to know, but on the demographic of the respondents as well. This follows, especially, in self-administered surveys where the questionnaires are given directly to people for completion. In this, the survey needs to be clear, following topics in order, with clear and concise directions in answering the questions.

Fink and Kosecoff address the issue of sample size but recommends questions that the survey authors should consider: how quickly is the data needed, what type of survey is planned, what are your resources, how credible will you findings be, and how familiar are you with sampling methods. The advantages of random sampling are that the survey authors are able to choose a sample that represents various groups and patterns of characteristics in the desired proportions—age group, faculty, staff, students, and other demographics as pertinent. That is, the surveyors divide the entire group into subgroups and take a sampling from these. Fink and Kosecoff suggest at least 20–30 persons from each subgroup.

Once a survey has been designed in print, it will not take much effort for conversion to an electronic format; the easiest, of which, is email based. By using a cgi script and a web-based form, surveys may be filled out online. When this form is submitted, results are sent to a predetermined email address. A database-driven form could be set up to take input and organize by fields. In this, the results could also be automatically calculated, with entire results displayed in a report. This can be done with an off-the-shelf package such as Microsoft Access. This method takes more time setting up, but will be better suited to handle large numbers of submissions. For a survey set of less than a couple hundred, email is an easier option. The results in the body of the email should be set up in a delimited fashion to allow copying and pasting into a spreadsheet or statistical program. The results are then tabulated within the software.

While there are many surveys available, there may be greater value in creating one that speaks directly to the individual library and its users. The locally created survey will assume no generalities (unless needed) and give the authors are freer range on the types of issues the survey is to address. It may be worthwhile to have a few variations on surveys to different audience members—that is, faculty, staff, students, as each has specific needs that will differ from the other subgroups.

This information can then be housed in a digital library. An open source digital graphical system is the foundation for original and collaborative knowledge content development for partnerships. Digital libraries are online information environments offering access to a multitude of resources and digital services. As will any typical brick-and-mortar library, digital libraries attempt to cultivate and organize collections and services into a useful integrated location. In this, the new libraries are not single entities; these libraries allow many links to other digital libraries offering almost complete access to collections, including items that cannot be displayed or distributed on paper (i.e., audio and video). Digital libraries connect not only sundry and dispersed collections, but also the evolving range of online communities. In this, digital libraries are less recognized for their collections than their access to the online communities. This knowledge will be the product of the Techheads research and collaboration. The system is a natural extension of research collaboration and authority of information created at the organization or school level. The users and facilitators of this system will be faculty, staff, students, librarians, and technical staff.

Finally, the Techheads will see some key areas in which to begin, with particular buy-in from those who had been invited to participate in survey completion and discussions. Once a focus has been decided, the group should frame the agenda while maintaining an open relationship to everyone engaged. This fosters trust while encouraging others to be involved.

For your interest, we have included a draft survey that you may find useful for your own projects in Appendix A.

Staff Development: Project-Based Learning

Markham et al., describe Project Based Learning as emerging over the past 25 years through research in neuroscience and psychology as these have extended cognitive and behavioral models of learning illustrating that thinking, doing, and the contexts of learning are intimately tied. Learning, they maintain, is partly a social activity taking place within the context of past experience, culture, and community. How might the Techheads use this in staff development? They continue that learners not only respond to the feedback of information, but also actively use what they know to explore, interpret, and create. Students construct solutions, shifting the emphasis toward the process of learning. The authors also maintain that teachers understand that the world is changing, and as such, education needs to adapt to this changing world utilizing new instructional practices that reflect the students' new environment using standards-focused projects using the following criteria:

- Recognizing students' inherent drive to learn and putting them in the center of the process
- Engaging students in the central principles and concepts
- Highlighting provocative issues that lead to in-depth exploration
- Ensuring the requirement of using essential tools and skills for learning and knowledge management
- Specifying products that solve problems through research and critical thinking
- Including multiple products that permit frequent feedback
- Using performance-based assessments that communicate rigor, challenges, and high expectations
- Encouraging collaboration

While Markham et al., admit that there is not sufficient evidence to assert that Project Based Learning is a proven alternative to other educational forms, they do state that there are data that show that Project Based Learning enhances the quality of learning while leading to higher-level cognitive development from engagement with complex problems. This is a good model for our Techheads. At the very least, we can say that all types of learners have better luck with technology implementation or utilization if they are using the thing that they are learning, while they are learning the thing; that is, if a class is going to learn Photoshop, have the class use Photoshop using their own images while they are learning the software and techniques. At the very least, they will having something to take with them that they have tangibly used within the context of their learning.

How Does This Translate to Techheads?

At this point in your project, you should have your survey completed and compiled with responses, drafts, correspondence, and other materials posted in your digital library. Your project outline and requirements should be in place using the Technology Implementation Request and Technical Evaluation Forms. We would like to share with you a real Project Based Learning project that has been completed with some current students. This is a really good example of implementation.

Last year it was decided that the Student Center would initiate some technology upgrades to the building. Without going into all of the details, the project was to upgrade all of the conference rooms to a basic standard technology capability. As above, it was decided, based on the size of the rooms, to install wall-mounted TVs with cabling for any type of device connection. After quotes were initially received, it was discovered that the department could save about $20,000.00 in installation fees alone if the installation was handled internally. This was made a student project.

With an initial direction of what was wanted of the student crew, they were asked to come up with a plan. Because of the familiarity of the building itself and its use, the department relied on internal expertise rather than conducting a survey. The TVs were purchased from an outsourced provider. The department also saved about $100.00 per mount from our original quotes by purchasing the mounts from Monoprice.com; we purchase all of our mounts and most of our cables from them. While the team waited on the equipment to arrive, the student crew met regarding in-room cabling. Firstly, building administrators wanted to see what they would come up with in a system where all of the cables connecting to the TVs would reside in the room, but could be hidden when not in use. Secondly, all of the cables were to be wrapped in cable wrap to serve as a sort of umbilical from the media devices to the TVs. In this, there would always be a clean setup and not have to make any last-minute runs in hunting down connectors. One of the students built a prototype. It was a perfect first try. He made a small cabinet that would be installed in the wall under the mounted TV. This way, the umbilical cabling would come straight down, through the wall, and could be kept wrapped up in the box when not in use. He also cut a hole in the door so that the appropriate length could be taken out of the box and the door shut behind—very useful, very clean.

Before the equipment started to arrive, it was a task to book our Physical Plant and our cable provider to add outlets to the appropriate locations that would be behind the TVs. Physical Plant installed electrical outlets that are switched with Levitron keys from a wall plate near the TVs. This is a policy choice as the policies require those who reserve a room to request equipment for the space; the power is switched on and off as is appropriate to the request. The cable TV provider also installed cable jacks in locations near the power.

The TVs arrived (mostly 55" though a few 60") and property tagged. The crew started the mounting process. The student crewmembers were able to knock these out in about a day—two if they had to wait on varnish to dry on the boxes. The crew mounted plywood directly to the wall studs, cut appropriate holes for the cabling, attached the back of the TV mount to the plywood, the front to the TV, ran the umbilical down the wall, hung the TV on the wall, leveling as necessary. They tested each mount by hanging on it like you would a pull-up bar. Lastly, another student would come in after to pull the umbilical through the box, attach the box to the wall, wrap, and lock it up. A quick dusting and vacuum, and the room was completed. The crew tested each room's installation by plugging in various media players, such as laptops and Blu-ray player to test the connections. Finally, a little break with ESPN on the TV and we called it finished. The students did a great job, at least as professional as the company installers that we had hired. The installation was solid, and again, the department saved almost $20,000.00.

Evaluating for Ongoing Success

It is essential at the outset of any project to determine the approach, the expectations, and the methodology, including possible instruments, within the constructs of the focus previously determined.

The evaluation may consist of examining processes, costs and benefits, and impacts of the project. Process measures should include documentation of routine project activity, such as faculty participation in workshops; workshop evaluations; number and date of instructional media submissions by faculty, staff, and students; requests for equipment; relinquishment of equipment; student enrollment in the workshops; number of approved productions resulting from class projects; student evaluation of teaching; and the like. The group should also track the costs of conducting the proposed project, which typically include personnel time, costs of operation (supplies, blank media, etc.), and equipment repairs. Benefits and expectations could include the volume of product or training accessible to students, while measures of volume, accessibility, and policy compliance may be multidimensional. The impact assessment will report the number of clients served by the project and evaluation of material. Faculty reports of their experiences with this project should also be compiled along with the total volume of instructional or other material produced through the project. Perhaps the most important and complex impact measure will be developed to assess the appropriateness of its intended audience.

Providing appropriate and clear standards within the project is critical in communicating expectations and providing a measurable benchmark to assess the quality of the project. But setting standards represents a major challenge; as such, activity must consider both student learning styles and content.

The team should decide how far an assessment approach will take over the course of this project and into the future. During the initial stages of the project, conduct a study of learning styles and strengths across the department. Establish from this study the modes of presentation that have the highest impact upon participants. With this information in hand, participants will become involved in defining issues related to subject matter and developing models of instruction that are well suited to various types of subject matter. As we had discussed earlier in this book, by allowing participants to bring their own materials into the equation, they have a more firm foundation as they are able to put the new information into a context they already understand while having new materials to work with after the project or workshop. It is important that clientele participants representing the range of areas are involved in this process. Through the workshops, establish a set of models representing different levels of accomplishment in matching learning styles within the project scope. This assessment instrument will rate the degree to which a given submission meets students' learning profile and the content within a given area.

It is our belief that beginning a Techheads group where representatives from the technology and library departments share in offering Project Based Learning opportunities for the institution as a whole will foster collaboration in other areas and other projects, including grant applications. This can only be good for all involved.

Summary

In engaging others to participate in and with the Techheads group, it is important to express the proposal in a meaningful way. The tools that we have shared with you will assist you in creating a narrative.

1. Survey your clientele

2. Create your narrative

3. Find your space

4. Share your space

5. Plan your project

6. Use your project to train about your project

7. Evaluate your project

We believe these steps will not only assist in creating a great collaborative team, but also give you the tools to successfully implement new projects of any size, and undertake and foster a greater collegiality between librarians and technologists.

Works Cited

Bell, M. A., et al. (2006). "Distance Learning Content Sharing" in *Cybersins and Digital Good Deeds*. Philadelphia: Haworth Press.

Fink, A, J. Kosecoff (1998). *How to Conduct Surveys: A Step-by-Step Guide.* Thousand Oaks, CA: SAGE Publications.

Jones, D. (1997). "Plays Well with Others; or, the Importance of Collegiality in a Reference Unit." *Reference Librarian*, 59, 163–175.

Lorenzen, M. "Collegiality and the Academic Library" in *Electronic Journal of Academic and Special Librarianship* 7, no. 2 (Summer 2006). Retrieved March 4, 2013, from http://southernlibrarianship.icaap.org/content/v07n02/lorenzen_m01.htm.

Markham, T., J., Mergendoller, J., Larner, and J., Ravitz. (2003). "Introduction to Project Based Learning." *Project Based Learning Handbook.* (2nd revised/special edition, pp. 3–8). Novato, CA: Buck Institute for Education. Retrieved March 4, 2013, from http://www.bie.org/store/item/pbl_handbook/.

Van Roekel, James. "Beyond Daily Set-Up: Student Crewmembers as a/v Installers" in *The Bulletin of the Association of College Union International* (July 2012).

Epilogue

Change happens, and in technology, this occurs with dizzying speed. In Chapter 1, we take a look back at the history of technology in schools. In education, the adage once was that change occurs very slowly. This is no longer the case and will not be a viable future view. As discussed in Chapter 1, there were developments over many years leading up to the current fast-moving world of technology in all aspects of our society. Certainly since the 1980s, things have accelerated to a near-breakneck pace as far as technology is concerned. Looking back and reflecting on the distance from life in the 1980s as contrasted with today's life provides a backdrop for the information offered in this book. While the profession of librarianship has been around for thousands of years, the rise of techheads is fairly recent, at least if one defines them as people who work with computers. These two groups of professionals, librarians and technology specialists, need to work together today in schools more than ever before. Now is the time to make this happen.

School librarians collaborate with teachers and other librarians to facilitate student learning that integrate technology. Their unique role is discussed in Chapter 2. During the lessons, they assist students with the use of the technology rather than allowing the technology to overtake productivity. The results of students' learning are products designed to be shared with others. Many students are already collaborating on-line outside of school using social networking. Educators attempt to connect with students' interests by using what the students know and use in the learning process. However, thought regarding the selection of the tools should include what the tool is able to do and provide for the students' learning experience.

In Chapter 3, we focus on technology specialists. The models of McLuhan and Wyatt point out that in our information society, the notion of a tribal culture has morphed. Clients now have access to the same tools technologists have, albeit varying skill levels. However, it is the technology that morphs the culture. Facebook, for example, might be thought of as a tribe. We introduced the idea of creating a knowledge management plan and infrastructure as well as techheads group calling for across-the-institution communication and collaboration among interested parties. By thinking in new ways, we are able to better assist our clientele and our colleagues.

Chapter 4 deals with the ways both librarians and techheads work with and for students. Parents hold concerns about their children's online safety. School librarians can help educate parents about online safety for their children through family literacy events, school newsletters, links on the Parents page, and informal conversations with parents who call or stop by the library asking questions. The idea is for parents to help their children practice online safety and to create a safe online environment for their children at home. At school, the Acceptable Use Policy (AUP) defines how technology should be used for educational purposes. The AUP is designed to provide safety for students. In addition, it also lets students know their responsibilities when they are online at school. While restrictions are placed on Internet use by students in the school environment, school librarians collaborate with teachers to bring the best technology tools to students for use with their learning. However, it is the students' learning that must drive the selection of the technology. Otherwise, the technology will override the learning process. In order to overcome this, having students solve problems that are based on real-life situations, the students will then select the appropriate technology to use for their learning and the resulting product that they will create from the experience.

As in any relationship, someone needs to take the first step to improve a situation that is less than desired. Chapter 5 is about building bridges. It really does not matter whether it is the librarian or the techhead who reaches out first, but someone needs to do it. As previously mentioned, the acronym for the word REACH can be summarized as follows:

R = Respect counterparts.

E = Educate yourself regarding the role of the individual with whom you want to build a bridge.

A = Assume responsibility as the one to reach out. Do not wait or tell yourself it will never work.

C = Communicate and collaborate!

H = Help one another to provide the very best instruction and experiences for students.

Taking the first step and continuing to follow through really is not optional any more. In today's hard times, educators must work together for the sake of their students.

As previously mentioned, the techheads group should strive to "play well with others," and Chapter 6 explores this further. The notion of collegiality, according to Jones, which seeks an environment that is conducive to working together effectively, is an important first step for collegiality, by promoting trust and inclusiveness, and increasing job satisfaction and deferring competitiveness, envy, and dictatorial supervision. Chapter 6 uses jazz as a metaphor to discuss collegiality and the primacy of the song, or project, before individuals. We also discussed a few ideas on survey utilization and a few real-world assessment tools to evaluate the collaborative programs and the educational outreach that come from these.

The time to have separate domains with different and sometimes opposing values and goals is long past. All educators need to work together to provide the very best for students. We hope that this book encourages increased collegiality, communication, and collaboration between librarians and techheads. The present fast-moving world of technology can only accelerate. Working together is essential and will continue to be so in the future.

Appendix A: Library Use Survey

*use in conjunction with forms to assist in defining your project

What is your campus affiliation?

———— Student

———— Faculty

———— Staff

What is your student status?

———— Freshman

———— Sophomore

———— Junior

———— Senior

During a typical week, how often do you visit the Library?

———— More than 5 times a week

———— 4–5 times a week

———— 2–3 times a week

———— 1 time a week

From *School Librarians and the Technology Department: A Practical Guide to Successful Collaboration* by Mary Ann Bell, Holly Weimar, and James Van Roekel. Santa Barbara, CA: Linworth. Copyright © 2013.

———— Less than 1 time a week

———— Never

Why do you not visit the Library? (Check all that apply)

———— Do not use/not aware of the services offered

———— No time

———— No interest

———— Other (please specify) ————————————————————

Why have you visited the Library in the past? (Check all that apply)

———— Hang out on my own

———— Hang out with friends/socializing

———— Study

———— Use computers

———— Attend a meeting

———— Wireless internet

———— Attend programs/events

———— Seek information

———— Other (please specify) ————————————————————

What would you like to see offered in the Library to get you to visit?

———— More seating in common areas

———— Quiet/private areas

———— Additional meeting rooms

———— More information for student opportunities

———— Greater accessibility

———— Additional technology

———— Other (please specify) ————————————————————

From *School Librarians and the Technology Department: A Practical Guide to Successful Collaboration* by Mary Ann Bell, Holly Weimar, and James Van Roekel. Santa Barbara, CA: Linworth. Copyright © 2013.

How many events have you attended in the Library in the last semester?

——— 0

——— 1

——— 2

——— 3

——— 4

——— 5 or more

Please indicate the times on the following days and times you would be most likely to attend an event held at the Library.

Please indicate the days you would be most likely to attend a Library event: (Check all that apply)

——— Monday

——— Tuesday

——— Wednesday

——— Thursday

——— Friday

——— Saturday

——— Sunday

Please indicate the times you would be most likely to attend a Library event: (Check all that apply)

——— 8 a.m.—11 a.m.

——— 11 a.m.—2 p.m.

——— 2 p.m.—5 p.m.

——— 5 p.m.—8 p.m.

——— 8 p.m.—10 p.m.

What promotions are most effective in making you aware of Library services or events? (Check all that apply)

——— Wall banners

——— Mail flyers

——— Framed posters in the Library

——— Digital Signage

——— Website

——— Individual programming schedules/calendars

——— Signs

——— Facebook/Social Media

——— Other (please specify)

Do you have any additional comments or suggestions?

——— Yes (please share)

——— No

Contact Name, Title

        Office: xxx.xxx.xxxx

user@email.edu

        Fax: xxx.xxx.xxxx

Appendix B:
Technical Evaluation Checklist

The xxxx Techheads provide leadership and support to the institution's initiative to enhance teaching and learning through skillful integration of technology in the learning process. The Techheads group is a resource for institution faculty and students in all classes, providing guidance and expertise in developing a wide range of technology enhanced and online instruction and projects. The Techheads identifies and evaluates equipment and software for potential utilization within the institution and training needs for faculty and students to assist them in incorporating appropriate technology in their classes. In this, the Techheads gives technical consultation prior to the design and evaluation prior to the implementation of technology or content:

1. The course audience has been identified.

While this is an issue for the department and school, the Techheads recommend to the instructor that this issue be addressed prior to the design as utilizing technology for the content greatly depends on the goal of the project. This will be verbally verified with the designer prior to implementation.

2. The choice of technology is driven by the content.

That is, the technology fits the content,not, the content fits the technology. The technology has been chosen because it was the best delivery method for the content and how it is being shared or utilized.

From *School Librarians and the Technology Department: A Practical Guide to Successful Collaboration* by Mary Ann Bell, Holly Weimar, and James Van Roekel. Santa Barbara, CA: Linworth. Copyright © 2013.

3. The course is ADA compliant.

Per xxxx Policies and Procedures.

4. Electronic documents can be easily printed.

Users are able to print documents to allow for portability. Some prefer to view content in this fashion.

5. The course layout is easily navigated.

The Techheads verify that all hyperlinks are correctly connected. This includes, but is not limited to, clear access to the materials or electronic classroom: assignments, lectures, course materials, off-site materials, the library, student support, and instructor or project manager contact information.

6. Interactivity of the materials.

The Techheads verify student/student, student/instructor, and instructor/class interactivity. This will take place on many levels depending on the individual course. As a result, interactivity is judged on a project-by-project basis, in close collaboration with the instructor or designer. Interactivity may include, but is not limited to, chat rooms, email, discussion boards, and telephone.

7. Media.

As online content continues to grow in popularity, and as electronic media becomes easier and less expensive to create, instructors will rely more heavily on this media in delivering content to students. The use of media in classes or projects is a decision left to the instructor and the evaluation of content to the department. However, where used, the technical quality of the media will be evaluated. This includes, but is not limited to, clarity of audio, viewing and physical size of image and video, proper file size for streaming, and media broadcast file length.

8. Proper use of off-site and secondary resources.

The Techheads will work with instructors and the institution's copyright officer to verify permissions to use copyrighted materials on-site. Links and citations to off-site materials are an example or proper use.

9. Relative transparency of the technology.

Because of the primacy of the content, technology is used only as a tool. The Techheads will assist the designer and ensure that the use of technology does not hinder the dissemination of course content. The designer and the Techheads will evaluate this. If the Techheads find any of these aspects lacking, the group offers continued training and support to help designers meet the criteria.

Appendix C:
Technical Evaluation Checklist

1. The audience has been identified_____

2. The choice of technology is driven by the content_____

3. The material is ADA compliant_____

4. Electronic documents can be easily printed_____

5. The web layout is easily navigated_____
   Hyperlinks connected_____

6. Interactivity of the materials (students and faculty)_____
   Email_____ Chat Rooms_____ Discussion Boards_____ Telephone_____

7. Media_____
   Text_____ Still Images_____ Audio_____ Video_____
   Appropriate file sizes_____

8. Proper use off-site and secondary resources_____
   Library materials_____ Off-site citations_____ Copyrighted materials_____
   (requires library director's signature)_____

9. Relative transparency of the technology_____

   I have reviewed_____.
These materials are easily navigable and contain appropriate interactivity. It
facilitates the proper use of off-site and secondary resources and maintains a
relative transparent use of technology. As such, I certify the use of technology
in this project. If prior compensation agreements have been made between the
faculty member course developer and academic department chair, I recommend
that

_____ be compensated for the development
of these materials.

_____
               Signature   Date

Additional signatures may be required per policy.

_____
               Signature   Compensation AMT*   Date

Appendix D: Techheads

Agenda

DATE

Old

Media Style Sheets

TSUS/Campus Policies regarding class recording

Video: Flash, storage, formats, archive, workflow

Second Life

    NETnet programs

    New

    Steve C's Shop

Appendix E:
Technology Implementation Request

Name of Requestor_____ Date of Request_____

Proposed Project Start Date _____ Proposed Project End Date _____

Contact Email _____Contact Phone_____

Proposed Project Title_____

    Please complete the following:

1. Describe the project

2. Describe the audience for the project and how the need was determined

3. How does the proposed project support the institution's mission

From *School Librarians and the Technology Department: A Practical Guide to Successful Collaboration* by Mary Ann Bell, Holly Weimar, and James Van Roekel. Santa Barbara, CA: Linworth. Copyright © 2013.

4. How will the project be evaluated and what instruments will be used

5. Will there be any outside contractual agreements and how will these be documented

6. Present the budget for the proposed project and include how financial resources will be secured

Requestor_____

                         Signature   Date

Techheads Representative_____

                         Signature   Date

Administrative Approval_____

                         Signature   Date

Index

Monitoring, 12, 30, 57
Motivation, 36, 37, 59, 61, 64–67
Moursund, David, PhD, 8

Net Day, 6, 10
Networking 5, 6,

Online conferences, 78
O'Reilly, Tim, 11

Palmer, Parker, 32
Papert, Seymour, 2
Parents, 2, 10, 12, 23, 28–29, 30,
    33, 34, 56–57, 58–59, 65, 64, 81,
    100
Podcasts, 38, 78
Postman, Neil, 77
Prezi, 11
Professional development, 16–17,
    26–27, 35, 62–63, 66, 80
Project Based Learning, 94, 95, 98
Project, 25, 46–48, 51–53, 65, 66, 77,
    78, 84, 87–88, 90–91, 93–97, 98,
    101, 107–8, 110, 113–14; collab-
    orative, 34, 55, 69, 85; inquiry,
    68

Responsible Use Policy, 55

School Library Media Specialist, 14,
    15, 23
School policies, 59, 61–63
Schrock, Kathy, 25, 84
Service(s), 29, 41–42, 46, 75
Shehan, John, 56
Sizer, Theodore, 26
SlideShare, 11, 66
"So what?", 48, 53, 89
Smartphone, 47, 51
Social networking, 34–35, 50, 56, 58,
    62, 99

Software applications, 24–25, 27, 28,
    34–37, 39, 57–58, 84
Student Handbook, 59
Student interest, 36, 38, 67
Suterland, Camille, 82

Takeuchi, Lori, 28–30
Techheads, 8, 13, 15, 19, 42, 47,
    50–53, 72, 85, 87–95, 97–101,
    107
Technological literacy, 55, 59
Technology; Audio/Video, 29, 49, 55,
    57, 115; Department, 24,
    26, 28, 36, 38, 41, 45, 47, 62;
    iPads, 59, 112, 113; iPods, 50;
    Thoughtware, 56; Two-way inter-
    active video, 55; TVs, 113, 118,
    119–20; Vocabulary, 55
Texas Computer Educators Associa-
    tion, 94
Texas Library Connection (TLC),
    78
Towle, Meagan, 79
Training, 14, 16–18, 34, 38, 41–42,
    51–56, 62–63, 76, 97, 107–8
Twitter, 41–43, 48, 62

U.S. Government, 60
U.S. Supreme Court, 60

Vigil, Marian Royal, 78
VoiceThread, 11, 66
Von Drasek, Lisa, 19–20

Warlick, David, 59
Web 2.0, 10–11, 78, 79, 80
Webinars, 62
WebMD, 55–57
Wikipedia, 11
Willard, Nancy, 59
Windows on Science, 5

About the Authors

MARY ANN BELL, EdD, Professor, Department of Library Science, Sam Houston State University. She has authored two books, *Internet and Personal Computer Fads* and *Cybersins and Digital Good Deeds*.

HOLLY WEIMAR, EdD, Associate Professor, Department of Library Science, Sam Houston State University.

JAMES VAN ROEKEL, MLS, MA, Associate Director, Lowman Student Center, Sam Houston State University, from December 2011 till present. He has written two books, *Internet and Personal Computer Fads* and *Cybersins and Digital Good Deeds*.

Made in the USA
Middletown, DE
28 October 2017